Promoting Your Business 2019

A starter guide to driving brand awareness and lead generation for your business using integrated communications: PR, PR+, social media marketing, influencer marketing, online advertising, modern search engine optimisation (neo-SEO), content marketing and event marketing.

by Ian Hainey

1. Foreword
2. Planning
3. Integrated communications
4. PR
5. PR+
6. Social media marketing
7. Influencer marketing
8. Online advertising
9. Neo-SEO
10. Content marketing
11. Event marketing
12. Epilogue
13. About the author
14. Contact the author
15. Acknowledgements

Copyright © 2018 by Integrated Holistic Communications. All rights reserved. This book or any portion thereof may not be reproduced or used in any manner whatsoever without the express written permission from the author, except for the use of brief quotations.

Foreword

Having worked in marketing in various forms and promoted businesses of many types and sizes over the past two decades, I have had the pleasure of speaking with countless directors of multinationals, smaller business owners and budding entrepreneurs looking to turn their business dream into a reality. As an integrated communications agency (some may refer to it a marketing agency) owner, I've encountered a proliferation of managers who wanted to recruit the services of an agency to handle all their marketing efforts, but either simply couldn't afford it or fully rationalise the potential benefit against the cost. However, not being in a position to pay a retained agency to handle your communications should never hold you back from harnessing the power of marketing in order to build your business.

Ergo, I have been toying with the idea of writing this book for some time. Through the content of this book I will deliver for you the reader, an extensive working knowledge across several major and common marketing elements, which will help you to quickly understand simple disciplines that can transform a business' fortunes surprisingly quickly and to a budget. The more I thought about it, the more it made sense to get my experience down and share it with others. Therefore, I've written this book in a way that should give sufficient guidance to anyone looking to promote a business. You could be someone looking to take their existing business to the next level, or even just trying to get a better insight into marketing – or what we call 'integrated communications', where we largely avoid the use of expensive traditional advertising. It might help you better understand the foundations before you consider investing in a consultant, agency or adding in-house resources to deliver these functions. In fact, I wish I had read something like this early on in my own career and am sure it will help students, interns, juniors or others considering this occupation to gain a better insight into what the job currently entails.

While researching this book, I read many other guides to the marketing areas covered, with the overwhelming feeling that so many of the business owners and busy executives I know would neither have the time nor patience to absorb their chatty style, nor find the academic textbooks practical enough to implement. With this in mind, I have attempted to keep this book as succinct as possible with the goal of making it optimally efficient - a crash course, if you like. In this book I have also spent less time than others dwelling on where the industry was, instead focusing on where it is in 2019 and the best tools for achieving your business objectives. I stayed clear of filling it with statistics, instead asking you to trust I have thoroughly researched all assertions made. Each chapter could be extended into its own book, but I hope you use them as a foundation to get yourself online and discover more, keeping abreast of new technology, guides and marketing software that can really make a difference to your business. I am confident this will provide an easy-to-follow and implementable overview and insight into the powerful integrated communication tools that should be considered and experimented with to surpass your targets.

Planning

"Whether you're planning a single marketing campaign or a major five-year plan to propel your brand to number one, the key to success is planning. Simplistically, it's a case of 'rubbish in, rubbish out'. Or, as we used to say at Domino's: 'train hard, fight easy'. And that's the crux of it, the more thought that goes into any project, the more prepared you'll be to implement it with confidence and the better equipped you'll be to circumvent the ultimate changes and curveballs that always appear out of thin air. If you spend the time up-front considering all the potential ways to achieve your objectives; develop a brilliant but simple strategy and get as much detail down as possible, then you can manoeuvre better as a stronger team with more confidence, creativity and freedom. Therein lies the second most important part of the puzzle; ensuring that everyone in the company knows what it is you're actually setting out to do. Get the plan right plus the whole team behind it and you'll never look back," Chris Moore, former CEO, Domino's Pizza Group.

I almost published the book without this section – the irony of such poor planning. However, I later decided to add a chapter about planning because I simply believe it is the most important stage for promoting your business successfully. So many times, I have stressed the importance to my team of putting in extra time up front with a new client account to build a comprehensive initial strategy. The best reasoning I can give for doing this is: once the plan is agreed and in place, then anxiety levels drop, confidence rises and, most importantly, much of the hard work is already done. This allows you to execute delivery more effectively and with more creativity and flair. Structuring your plan can be aided by considering these three Cs:

Customers
Time should be spent analysing your customer – the 'dry stuff', such as their demographics, locations, interests, languages and potential contact points. Consider if your customer is also the end-user and, for business-to-business communications, understand who all of the stakeholders are. Get it all down, write it out with any research, projections and estimates necessary in order to document this crucial element, as only once you fully understand your clientele, can you communicate effectively with them. Also take the time to consider what motivates them, what they will spend time watching, listening to and reading on a regular basis and how you can communicate in a way that doesn't make them feel like they are being 'sold to'.

Have a look at your current customers – how did you attract them and why did they choose your company over all the competition out there? Then you can look at the customers of your competitors – why have they chosen to opt for their business instead of yours? You should consider the potential customers out there that don't know about or haven't yet found your company - we want to reach them all at least once. The general premise behind the way integrated, holistic communications approaches customers is through providing information they will find useful, enjoy and engage with. Every time you feel you are crossing over the line and hard-selling something to your customers, then tread with caution and consider how you yourself feel when you are spammed with offers. However, on occasion you might just be able to create a successful promotional communication, if what you are selling is highly targeted, timely and genuinely an attractive offer.

Once you have established ways in which to communicate effectively with your target audience, you can then introduce and develop key messages about what makes your company different – the unique selling points (USPs) that could make a customer choose your company or product ahead of others. An example is what you are reading right now. Few would invest months or years in writing a marketing book to make money, but if they are like me, they are writing it as a way of helping many people achieve their goals at the same time. It also allows me to reach a much wider target audience than would be possible through only the single medium of a physical agency. Who knows what might then happen if someone reads to the end of the book and thinks 'that guy seems to have a good knowledge built up over two decades promoting businesses. If this happened, they might consider contracting me to help them promote their business, inviting me to speak at an event full of business owners, or simply follow me as a source of information, to enable them to stay ahead of the curve through future publications or marketing updates.

Channels
A company's website remains a crucial cornerstone for any business – it is the shop front and an all-important resource that should be maximised in terms of your performance on Google. We have promoted hundreds of clients over the years, but it is nigh-on impossible to have a huge effect on improving a company's online real estate if its website is not optimised or updated with the latest required technologies. In fact, we are with increasing regularity advising companies of all sizes that we need to knock down their website and build a new fit-for-purpose version before we can effectively optimise and market it across all digital channels. The good news is, a good standard of website can be created by nearly anyone relatively cheaply who has the time, using platforms such as WordPress and Wix, who also provide a user-friendly content management facility that can be learned and then easily updated going forward.

The website should be optimised, including landing pages created for each service or main department. Each page should have carefully chosen wording that tallies with the type of words potential customers would use in the Google search engine. While it is important to use relevant keywords throughout every page, the main headline must clearly describe the content of each page. Following this logic, use the most important keywords closer to the beginning of the heading – if checking out guides on this, you'll find the header is marked <H1> in the code. The headings and subheadings you use on each page should also contain keywords that directly relate to the text below them. If your site is a lead generation tool, then you should implement ways of capturing contact details from the traffic you are driving there, such as contact forms, a chatbot such as Zopim or Zendesk and lead capture pop-ups such as Optinmonster and Sumo.

It's also important to find ways to keep your website current and dynamic. For example, adding a news section or blog and imbedded social media feeds can instantly bring your business to life for visitors, which can attract more traffic and help it perform better on search engines. In the same way we are forever advising companies to delete social media accounts they are not willing to invest time in, the same goes for websites: if it looks like nothing is happening in the company, then this is not the message we wish to portray. Never underestimate the power of perception in marketing.

We will go into more detail on the strategy for your social channels later. However, there are fundamental questions you need to consider in terms of your overarching strategy, such as: 'Which social channels will I use?' And 'Which social platforms should I avoid?' There is no harm in holding off before committing to certain social media channels. It's much more important to ensure the ones you are using are servicing a purpose for your business. Put another way: it's better to do less and do it well. You don't want a potential customer researching your social pages before taking the plunge with your business and opting for a competitor because they have a slicker Facebook page, or there has been no Twitter or Instagram activity for three months.

Conversation

Within your strategy you should consider what you would like your company's tone to be and how you would like to converse with and engage your audience. Once decided and added to your strategy, this important, but often overlooked, step should provide consistency across all the channels you commit to. We recommend companies consider and break down their communication into three Tones, which can be used across communications strategies: Industry, Corporate and Product.

Industry Tone is where you want your company to stand against your competitors. Do you want your company to be perceived as more casual or conservative in the way it communicates to customers, whether through media, social media, advertising or the events it hosts? Will you be targeting a specific segment of the target audience? An obvious example of this in action would be Virgin Atlantic and British Airways. The former throws up colourful advertising and edgy PR images of Branson on the wing of planes with glamorous cabin crew as they launch routes in new countries. While the latter is the ultimate in conservative brands, right down to their brand colours and uniforms, despite the fact they directly compete for the same target audience and fly passengers to the same destinations. By establishing the tone of the brand right from the start, it is easy for the entire company to adopt and embrace the personality that is to be portrayed.

Corporate Tone relates to the company itself: its people; its objectives and the way it wishes to be portrayed both internally and to the outside world. Do you want the company to be seen as focused upon its employees, or with technological advancement; is it a friendly family business or a dynamic, aggressive corporate animal? They do not need to be mutually exclusive as some companies have grown rapidly and successfully while maintaining their people as a priority. How do you want the activities of the company to be promoted? Do you want to sing about every contract win, or milestone, or are there certain types of news that should be kept internal? A little time spent considering this can help add to your content strategy and clarify the direction and parameters for all involved.

<u>Product Tone</u> is a focus on the goods or services you are providing. Identify the USP for each, then bring them to life by building stories using specialist knowledge and creating content that would be of interest to the target audience. For example, if you have a specialist, high-spec motor mechanic garage, then perhaps appeal to car enthusiasts with interesting clips about modern car maintenance or make things fun with classic car model quizzes or far-out motoring trivia. Perhaps even have someone write a blog in a question and answer format with some opted-in customers being interviewed about their relationship with their car and some of the interesting places they have driven to. The beauty of communications is there are really no limits to your creativity and there are always ways to make any business interesting to its target audience.

This brings us nicely on to the topic of planning the creation of regular information to be hosted on your own website, such as news or blogging. If you want to be seen as an expert in your field, or you want your company to be seen as a leader in the market, then it shouldn't be too much effort to write or film a regular short blog which contains content that would be interesting to your target audience. Set yourself or your team deliverables on a weekly or monthly basis and then ensure the blog is promoted through your social channels and on your website. Also, it is important to direct as at least some advertising budget towards pushing the blog out to your target audience, as it is often difficult to generate any sort of engagement without this. And exercise some patience – a large percentage of people begin a blog with best intentions, but don't see results immediately, so stop doing it. You need to bear in mind it can take some time to gather momentum, and once someone finds and enjoys the content, they often go back and view the older stuff.

A few days or even hours considering these three C's at the outset will save you time and anxiety in the future and facilitate the potential to greatly improve the effectiveness of your communications. In addition, we have also already touched upon some important elements of search engine optimisation, which will inevitably stand your company in good stead in terms of developing some prime Google real estate.

Integrated communications

"The ethos of strategic integrated communications is ensuring the chosen promotional tools work together harmoniously in a concerted effort to deliver consistent messaging to the target audience from multiple channels to produce results far in excess of expectations for the given budget," **Ian Hainey, CEO, iHC.**

Integrated communications is a holistic approach to promoting a brand to potential customers and stakeholders through several channels, while maintaining consistent messaging. Through building and executing a strategic plan for your brand, driving main marketing disciplines, such as PR, social media, advertising and events through the same person, team or agency, this synergetic approach can produce more impactful and economical results.

Well, being an integrated communications agency owner, I would say that wouldn't I? However, look at it pragmatically: most marketing activity has the goal of increasing brand awareness, delivering certain messages and lead generation, so why would a silo approach to this ever be more effective? In addition, there are obvious economies of scale to be had through being able to resource all activities through one person, team or agency rather than lots of different parties.

When all tactics are considered from an integrated perspective it is easier to identify how each element can be leveraged and communicated most effectively. The integrated approach is by far the quickest way to grow your brand and do it the right way, while building credibility.

The first key question I ask in every new client meeting when discussing the concept of integrated communications is 'what exactly are your goals?' Shortly after we have all these laid out, we begin to focus on the customer by understanding who we are looking to communicate with, where they extract information, which networks they are part of and what they value. Then we align these two elements and build our integrated communications strategy around them. It might sound overly simple – well, it is when the time is taken to be strategic. In most cases, the better we establish these two elements from the outset, the more successful the communications strategy will be. Next, your budget, whether weekly, annually or monthly should be established and the deliverables are then adapted and prioritised to fit.

Spend some time considering your brand's story and USPs, then prioritise these elements from top to bottom and add these into the communications strategy. Sometimes referred to as a messaging hierarchy, this involves physically listing the key messages you wish to portray and the order of importance, which helps focus all future communications and acts as a document for all involved to refer to. When creating your message hierarchy, which can usually be compressed into only one page, always keep front-of-mind what makes this organisation, individual, product or service stand out from its competitors. Create your integrated communications plan, enact it, but be flexible and regularly monitor, evaluate and adjust.

PR

"We didn't have a big budget as a startup business, and effective, engaging PR has been the best way for us to get noticed for a fraction of the budget that big breweries set aside for marketing and advertising. By pushing the boundaries of what beer and business could be through creative PR, we have been able to drive global conversation and build our community. Our mission is to make other people as passionate about great craft beer as we are. PR has been a key component of building our community through inspiring storytelling via the media," James Watt, co-founder, Brewdog.

In marketing there are few things more effective and that can bring more credible exposure for your buck than a newsworthy, expertly-written and deftly pitched press release accompanied by an impactful picture. Do not for one minute think your business isn't big enough, or sufficiently interesting for PR. Every company has its own interesting stories and a competent PR professional can create stories for any company. Trust me, I was even once tasked with generating monthly media coverage for an oil industry offshore crane company. It's a PR professional's job to extract stories on a consistent basis, but then most business owners also could - if they regularly had the time to reflect on what's happening. To deliver successful PR for your business, you need to think of your organisation and what it does as if you were a journalist - considering what readers would be interested in from an objective perspective. As an integrated communications agency, we're big believers in the power of a strong story. Our monthly PR activity for clients is often built around a main story or angle we'll push out through media and influencer contacts, then out further still through social channels and online advertising. It's often these stories that elevate our clients' profiles far above that of their competition in terms of awareness and competitive share of voice.

So, you have devised a story for your business and have organised it in a document as best you can, but you are a little reticent to pitch it to a publication. Don't worry about bothering the editor based on the fear they might not like the story you are pitching. Get to know their publication first, offer to take them out for lunch to introduce yourself and company and discuss any potential future stories or partnerships. The best editors - and there are many great editors, as it's not easy to get to that position within a decent media outlet - can create a story relevant to their audience out of almost anything. Of utmost importance is pitching the story in the right way – don't waffle, just give the top-down facts. What editors cannot bear above all else is laziness and lack of preparation. PRs they have no relationship with, who pitch a story without even understanding the story, never mind having researched the publication they are pitching for, is the bane of their working lives.

While PR works for all types and sizes of organisation, it's much more effective if a business is doing something fresh, interesting and exciting in the market. An extreme example is the craft beer brewer, Brewdog, which has exploded as a company, from two guys selling beers from out of the back of their van in 2007, to 1,800 employees and 80 bars worldwide at the start of 2019 - and its PR machine has played no mean part in it. The driving force behind the success of Brewdog's PR is the bravery of its founders, James Watt and Martin Dickie, who I have been aware of for some time due to their PR exploits. Brewdog's owners are masters of using PR for delivering their messages and you can spend hours browsing through their PR stunts online, which have included: dropping toy 'fat' cats from a helicopter in London to celebrate achieving a crowdfunding record; launching a beer called Hello My Name is Vladimir that poked fun at Russia's ban on 'homosexual propaganda' ahead of the Winter Olympics and promoting their End of History ale by packaging it inside the bodies of dead animals – the list goes on. Brewdog is quite fearless, as it pushes ahead with controversial ways to get its brand into the media spotlight. Most recently it announced to the media it was launched its own airline claiming to be the world's first craft beer airline, complete with a slickly produced video clip, which hit the global headlines - at the time of writing this, the story had over 12,000 hits on Google. Take a moment to consider the fact that Brewdog simply makes beer - but it is consistently turning ideas into priceless global media coverage using PR-led integrated communications tactics.

While Brewdog is selling its products to the general public, PR can be just as effective with business-to-business communications. We have clients in the construction, engineering and technical industries who get doors opened, added to tenders and win multi-million-dollar contracts from articles and thought-leadership pieces we create, get published and then push out for them to their niche target audience and decision makers. Nearly all industries have trade titles that are read by collective target audiences, so never consider your company too niche or 'boring' to bother with PR.

A strong story can appear in print and on the website of publications read by your industry and potential customers. The social media feeds of that media will usually share your news, often to huge audiences. Online news can massively boost your SEO and online presence. You have the opportunity to share this valuable content on your website, then through your social media channels to your own audience, then to a new audience through targeted social and online advertising. When potential customers are researching which company to use, their first stop is often Google and the brand awareness, credibility and online legacy you have created there can be the difference between drifting into obscurity or getting a meeting to land that next deal.

Particularly with corporate PR, there's often the view that there 'isn't much to talk about'. This can be a common misconception among busy executives. As PR professionals, the people we're speaking with, or interviewing for content, are nearly always in senior roles and time short. They rarely have the headspace to take a step back and consider all the important and interesting work they're doing. This work is nearly always newsworthy for their niche target audience and, regularly, to a wider business audience. A good PR professional is highly skilled at digging out the golden nugget. They turn a conversation into precious stories that can engage an audience and disseminate a large number of important key messages about the company along the way.

Businesses can't necessarily be expected to know what's interesting about themselves or what the media would find interesting about them. PRs marry the key messages and reputations of businesses with what their target audience, and therefore the relevant media, is interested in. The best trick for organising your thoughts and sourcing the strongest news stories is to compartmentalise the three distinct categories the news topics fit into, which I call The Voices: Industry, Corporate and Product.

Industry Voice is opinion, commentary and predictions, or research and statistics relating to the industry as a whole, that will often be of interest to a broad range of media and readers. This type of PR is capable of generating the biggest returns in terms of coverage and, if you get it right, even the odd front page or page leader story. For example, we released a story from a financial compliance company called CCL, giving an expert opinion about the amount of money laundering he predicted was happening in a country, which went straight to front page of the national business news. Another we did for currency exchange, Travelex, on the most expensive cities in the world in which to celebrate New Year was one of the main stories of the day and led the nation's news agenda.

Corporate Voice covers stories about the organisation itself, whether it is a senior appointment, plans for expansion, annual returns or project wins. These can be of particular interest to trade media and an audience within the specific industry sector. They can also appeal to a broader audience if the news is considered 'big' enough. The simplest form of this type of PR would be senior appointments, where the release may seem boring to some, but it is actually very interesting in the respective industry media, whether Energy, Construction or IT. For example, we released news of the appointment of regional head of Zurich Insurance, which hit the usual insurance and finance media, but also led to a host of interview requests and impressive mainstream business publications, television and radio coverage, due to the fact the brand is so well-known.

Product Voice stories are focus upon the products and services of an organisation. These can be a tougher sell to media, so the key commercial messages often need to be embedded within a topic or piece of content that provides value to the reader. For instance, we promoted a study by Zurich about what the cost of putting your child through university would be 18 years from that date and it made national news headlines, regardless of the fact we mentioned Zurich's saving products in the release and all the broadcast interviews. The story was a means to an end of communicating to a huge audience and reminding them the importance of saving for their children's education.

Over time, your public relations strategy should tell the story of your business, the people leading it and the individual parts that make it successful. On occasions when there are quieter months in terms of news, a *proactive* PR firm can generate a topical feature angle to ensure consistency of messaging and that new audiences are being continuously reached. In addition, the best ambassadors for organisations are usually their own employees, so never underestimate the power of profile articles. They provide the opportunity for experts within the company to speak with authority as thought leaders in the market, which can inspire confidence in the brand.

PR is powerful as it builds the identity of the brand and adds to its equity and value – even more so with the searchability of all articles online. While at Sportlobster, the global media coverage we were delivering, from celebrity partnerships, to hitting key milestones as a new social network, were prevalent in every presentation to potential investors, as a way of demonstrating credibility and affirming why they should invest more money into the social network. Similarly, when it comes time for a company to be sold, one of the first points of due diligence is to perform thorough searches on the organisation.

A simple example of PR's ability to build real credibility is an experience we had recently with a construction consultancy client, for whom we generated an extensive project case study in the top aviation industry magazine, which detailed the client's work on a high-profile international airport terminal in Abu Dhabi. Several months later they asked us to procure several print copies of the magazine, which they proudly handed over to the selection panel during their pitch to win a sizeable contract building another country's new airport terminal. They won the contract and were convinced the glowing editorialised piece may just have given them the edge.

When we take on a new PR client, much of the creative work is done before anything is released. A brainstorming session will be scheduled, then a key messaging hierarchy created, which lays out the most important messages of the brand to be communicated through PR activity over time in order to demonstrate the brand's identity and values. It also ensures key characteristics and USPs are carried over into any communication with media, whether written, or spoken during interviews. Regardless of whether your business requires business-to-consumer (B2C) PR or business-to-business (B2B) PR, the communications strategy should always include these factors, highlighting what your service or product is and how it is making a difference to your customers.

In general people like to do business with brands and people they trust, and PR is a top performing method of promotion in this respect. Most PR output is editorialised, usually with a level of implicit endorsement from a third party - someone else is delivering the message, not the brand itself. Therefore, it can be arguably the most effective marketing tool for rapidly building trust and credibility.

The press release process
The cornerstone of the PR profession is the press release, which is a document you should always put together, in some form, if targeting multiple media with the one story. The mighty 'release' has not changed very much over the past 20 years, other than the fact we now hyperlink elements within releases, in case some online news channels publish with links, allowing us to benefit from the subsequent SEO benefits.

There are a number of rules to follow that can help put together a strong press release:

Ensure you have added all information required to answer the 5Ws & How (who, what, why, where, when, how) and then find the 'golden nugget' which is the main point or newsline in the story and stick to this story angle. Sometimes there are multiple exciting elements of a development you want to get across, but always pick your one hook. In most instances when it looks like there are two stories, you should wait and do another release at a later date – avoid shoe-horning newslines together in the one release, as it nearly always becomes confusing and often wastes a perfectly good opportunity for a separate future story.

If you are the expert to be quoted within the press release, then consider having someone else interview you and take down notes, in order to ensure there is an objective point of view and as much information as possible is included in the first draft. However, always consider bringing another person into the press release, particularly if their input would make it more attractive to an editor and potentially more newsworthy. If it is relevant to the story, it is often the case involving quotations from more parties in the story will also build credibility, as there is more than one person's opinion involved. For example, when we launched a police-led award-winning anti-vandalism campaign in the city of Aberdeen, UK, we added a quotation from the leader of the city council in the press release and involved them in the launch and news picture, which elevated the perceived importance of the campaign to be more than just another police issue.

When writing your press release, take a step back and write the article objectively, more as if you were a journalist than a business, leaving any opinions to the quotes. Of course, a press release is a document that takes skill to do to the highest standard and is something a PR professional hones over many years of writing. However, there is no reason why you can't give it your best shot. It is important the release is structured in such a way those who receive it will quickly have their attention grabbed, so much of the crucial information must be delivered as early as possible in the document. For traditional news releases, the 'inverted information pyramid' style is the most common format and the way most expect and prefer to receive a release. Basically, the most important and newsworthy information appears in the first few paragraphs, which is then backed up by supporting details, then usually a quote or two, followed by other related information that could be of interest. A major benefit of this structure is the time a busy editor needs to invest in finding the key, newsworthy points in your release is minimised.

If still unsure what your release should look like, then check out the structure of the way articles are written in the media outlet you most want your story to appear - then simply copy the style.

Once your release is ready to go, perform some online searches and find the correct journalist within each of the titles you are approaching with your release - then send them a personal note with the emailed release introducing yourself, your business, and explaining why it is relevant for them.

Create a hit list of your target media and pick up the phone to follow up on your release. Have a pitch already prepared as to why the story is interesting for them. However, consider the type of media it is. If it's a monthly magazine, they won't answer emails immediately, so give them sufficient time to get to your email. In contrast, if it is a news story, you may only have a window of the first half of the day to get the story across to the daily journalists before they make decisions at their daily news conferences. If your story appears in one major newspaper the next day, it's much less likely a competing newspaper will publish the story at a later date than its rival.

Consider exclusives or embargoed releases - if it is particularly important to get the story into one media outlet, then have a conversation with the editor before release and offer them the chance to do a bigger exclusive 'spread' on the story. You are more likely to achieve this if you give them the information early. This doesn't necessarily scupper the story in other outlets if you get the timings right. However, always be up-front about public release dates when offering an exclusive, as editors can have long memories if they feel they have been somehow deceived.

Be confident - remember it is not always the media doing you the favour. Bringing them a relevant and newsworthy story, presented to them in a succinct and timely fashion is exactly what most editors appreciate. In addition, don't be afraid to follow up after some time. Media can be a chaotic world and I've lost count of the times I've successfully followed up a story and it had just simply been forgotten. Usually if a journalist says they will run with your story, they eventually will in some form, particularly if you take the time to politely remind them.

One of the biggest frustrations I have with employees is 'passive PR' when they are reluctant to pick up the phone to pitch and chase. However, the requirement for this element in the process is compulsory for success. Busy media outlets receive hundreds of emails a day - I know because I have asked them - and spoken contact remains the best way to cut through the competition. Most seasoned editors actually enjoy a good pitch. I often open the conversation with something like, "Hi - do you have 30 seconds for a good pitch?" If you want to appear in any media and you have the right story for them at the correct time, the only things stopping you are a lack of determination or poor preparation.

A good PR stunts has got to be my favourite element of the profession. I even remember when starting out in the PR industry two decades ago, buying books on PR to learn more about the career and flicking forward for details on any PR stunts. While not relevant for all types of business, a stunt can generate powerful, memorable coverage if executed well. It doesn't even have to break the bank - the most creative and effective stunts usually don't. For example, UK high street baker, Gregg's, began generating media coverage from when it announced it would be hosting candlelit dinners on February 14, 2018. The company gained masses of national coverage due to the absurdity of the tongue-in-cheek idea the budget chain, famous for cut-price pastries and cakes, could pull off fine dining. The press release and media relations were accompanied by a well-planned integrated strategy, including choreographed video and social media activity.

They produced impressive publicity before, during and well after Valentine's Day, including regional media interviews with headlines like 'pasties with prosecco' and 'I went on a date to Gregg's'. I love the fun way a sometimes simple, silly PR stunt idea can generate vast awareness and coverage, so if you have an idea at the back of your mind that might work as a PR stunt, speak to a PR professional about it and you might be surprised when it becomes a reality and 'blows up' publicity-wise.

UK supermarket chain Iceland arguably stole the show in terms of PR stunts in the run up to Christmas 2018, with how it used a video condemning palm oil use and its resulting destruction of the habitat of orangutans. The story of the societally-important, tear-jerking animation being 'banned' when Iceland submitted it for broadcast approval hit global headlines, with the world up-in-arms without fully understanding the background. Clearcast, which approves ads for British broadcasters said it couldn't pass the advert because 'political' advertising is not allowed in the country. Iceland didn't even create the ad, which is in fact a short animation that had been previously hosted on Greenpeace's website. Digging deeper, it transpires Iceland had in fact been found to score worst of all the major UK supermarkets for stocking products containing palm oil by a campaign group. The supermarket had indeed only claimed it would remove palm oil from all its own-brand foods in the future. Once Iceland had received its - likely expected – rejection letter from Clearcast, it promptly proceeded to post about it on its YouTube channel and on Twitter, with the message: 'You won't see our Christmas advert on TV this year, because it was banned. But we want to share Rang-tan's story with you… Will you help us share the story?' This, of course, sparked widespread outrage at this bureaucratic crime against nature. Within a month of the story breaking, there had already been several million YouTube views; a tweet with six-figures in both likes and retweets and shares from some of the world's biggest celebrities and superinfluencers. It quickly became the top story across major UK news media – then internationally it became a major trending story, as the world learned about this mere supermarket chain championing a fragile species' cause against the system. A Change.org petition was launched to have the clip cleared for television, which had approaching a million signatures when this was written. You can make your own mind up as to whether Iceland has pulled off one of the most effective PR stunts in history by exploiting a cause, the system and the emotions of the public to their own benefit, despite itself being a contributor to the problem. What's for sure is, if evaluated in terms of a PR stunt generating publicity and costing very little, if anything – it must be right up there. The content has already had much higher levels of engagement than it could ever have expected if it had been passed by Clearcast and Iceland had then paid the large costs of running it as a national television advert – it is all 'earned' coverage.

PR+

"From my experience PR is a powerful function to influence and engage audiences. In today's world many stories are first seen online. PR can therefore work best when it's complemented by other functions of the marketing mix, especially social media, which provides the opportunity to share the editorial, we work so hard to get, with a wider and highly-targeted audience," Megan Landauro, PR Manager, ING.

We use the term 'PR+' within iHC to encapsulate the switch to strategic and targeted PR, which then must be pushed out to the target audience over social media channels. I am an avid reader of media and I have worked on a news desk and written for national titles. I fondly recall stories of the halcyon days of a huge newsroom packed with talented writers and aggressive hacks. I remember the female senior crime writer during my stint at the Aberdeen Evening Express saying to me on the drive back from shadowing her all day at court: 'What we need, Ian, is a good murder'. Or the curmudgeonly business editor who referred to me as the tea boy as he mercilessly destroyed my submitted copy. I was in awe of some of these finely-honed story machines and consumed every inch of newspaper editorial they worked hard to produce. However, recently I caught myself reading a feature, which I wrote in a national newspaper - on my phone, clicked from the newspaper's Twitter feed, while the pristine paper version lay unopened beside me with my coffee mug on it.

We simply need to deliver PR+ because PR alone is no longer enough. Getting the PR team in the office to read the daily newspaper has proven a fruitless task. 'Why will you not even have a quick flick through the hard copy each day? It's important to see the journalist names, the weekly sections they write. Enjoy and be at one with the newspaper, which is indeed a product so important for your career', I prompt, while waving the newspaper at them. They furtively acknowledge me, too polite to tell me to stop bothering them, or laugh at me because they only take their news from social feeds.

Traditional media: proper titles with journalists, editors, sub-editors, designers, advertising team, etc, is still as important as it ever was. In fact, there is an argument that trustworthy, professional media is even more important now, with myriad new online news sites and influencers popping up and printing unsubstantiated and non-regulated 'news'. Most readers are not completely gullible but finding information on a site that has an enormous following, high page ranking, burgeoning social media and hundreds of comments on each story will more often than not be accepted as the truth.

Most research shows social media advertising has already overtaken advertising in print newspapers globally. However, the important thing to remember is: just because people aren't consuming print at the same levels anymore does not mean the articles are not being read as much. On the contrary, having information in one place means content is much more accessible for readers and globally searchable. Every piece of content published online has the potential to be much more valuable to society, read more often and in turn, worthy of more advertising spend.

As an agency, we made moves and adapted our model to PR+ several years ago, with much of our operations remaining PR-driven. Our agency has strong writers on board, but now there is a large digital team managing a smooth system of information flow through social media and digital advertising. It is a formula that works, as we have grown our retained client base steadily over the past few years, while other agencies have struggled. Recently there have been some well-publicised examples of large agencies making drastic personnel changes, as they are clearly restructuring to try and achieve similar aims. However, we firmly believe our success, in a challenging transitional period for the industry, has largely been down to our PR+ ethos. Generating fantastic media coverage is all well and good, but it's then what you do with it that really makes a difference.

The overwhelming feedback from clients in recent years is that they are increasingly seeing their articles being clicked and read more by the audience they actually want to be reading their key messages. They are even receiving messages from their target audience, giving thanks for the 'informative piece' or congratulating them on their (Industry, Corporate or Product Voice) news. Most importantly, of course, clients can now see a more tangible return on investment, in the form of new business enquiries, than in days when only traditional PR existed, because they can be contacted directly after reading an article or watching a news clip on social media, at touch of a button.

An example of PR+ in action is a global project management company we represent internationally. The regional director called me to excitedly explain how he had just had an extraordinary moment in a meeting, when a key decision maker from one of the country's main developers approached him to say he had enjoyed reading his magazine article on LinkedIn. The article, which featured the regional director, had been published in a key trade magazine through work by our PR team, then the social media team had posted the link to the article on the client's company LinkedIn, before advertising it on a pay-per-click basis to the client's target audience. This key person had never engaged with him before, never mind thanked him for putting together an interesting thought leadership piece had been one of the people the article had been advertised to reach. Fast forward six months and the client landed its biggest ever contract in the region worth millions of dollars with, you've guessed it, the very same developer.

In most developed countries, the majority of people are now receiving their news from their social media feeds. Consider how you stay on top of current events: on a daily basis do you, your colleagues and friends keep track of the daily news from your social feeds, by logging in to news sites, or picking up a newspaper? It can easily be argued that it is more important to get an article on the social media channels of most media outlets than the media's actual website, so how brands can be happy with generating coverage that has never been pushed out over social media is an ongoing mystery to me. Do not ignore the social media push-out of your hard-earned PR coverage, as you are wasting the opportunity to utilise some of the most powerful, relevant content around and deliver it to a much bigger and, in some cases, more targeted audience.

Consider which blogs and influential social media sites you should target. Who is assigned to pushing out your online PR coverage, how much budget will you put behind each story and on which channels and to which target audience? Create this plan not only for monthly activity, but for every campaign or event you do. If you don't plan these things in advance, you can miss the boat when your news passes its sell-by-date.

The last few decades have not seen the PR industry shrink as some may suggest. In fact, they have opened up a world of opportunity to deliver messages directly to more of your audience's devices and laptops – if tackled strategically and holistically. It is a truly exciting time for companies and agencies, as they have so much more power at their fingertips to deliver powerful PR+ that not only improves brand awareness but can make a real difference to your bottom line.

Social media marketing

"Social media promotion is major component of the marketing strategy for our veterinary business. We leverage the appeal of our furry patients by making them the stars of our monthly campaigns. Engagement is extremely high in our Facebook group and competitions attract hundreds of entrants and thousands of impressions, most of whom are exactly within our target audience. We foster a real feeling of community among our social media followers, which has an ongoing positive effect on our patient numbers and bottom line," Dr Sara Elliott, owner and director of veterinary services, British Veterinary Hospital.

We went on a family holiday to Koh Phi Phi in Thailand, the pristine white sand island setting for The Beach, a 1996 Alex Garland novel and 2006 movie starring Leonardo DiCaprio. The journey involved a taxi to the airport, flight to Bangkok, then connecting flight to Krabi, minibus to the water boat, which we then loaded with our suitcases and then unloaded on Koh Phi Phi's beautiful white sand beach. After some time standing in the blazing sun, a tractor took our bags to the hotel and after all that exhausting travel, we eventually made our way to the stunning infinity pool overlooking the Andaman Sea. There were nine people already at poolside and seven of them were not looking at the breathtakingly beautiful view, but firmly staring into their handsets, mainly updating and checking their social media feeds - I checked because I wanted to use the observation in an upcoming presentation. The point is: no matter where your target audience is, this is where most are looking, and the good news is that it makes it relatively cheap and simple to reach the right people with your messages.

Promoting your business properly on social media should not be a choice, but a compulsory activity for almost every type of organisation. Believe it or not, our agency even handles communications across the Middle East and Latin America for one of the world's superpowers, which uses social media alongside traditional media to raise brand awareness and communicate to decision makers in the many countries it targets to sell aircraft and military equipment.

Never lose sight of the fact a common route for people planning to do business with an organisation is to check its website and then click on its social media icons to see what it has been doing recently. When they check a Facebook, Instagram, LinkedIn or Twitter page and there is nothing there, or even just a few half-hearted posts a month, it can portray a lacklustre impression of the organisation. I've lost count of the number of times I have met with a potential new client and recommended they either delete unused platforms or begin using them properly. We are not talking about corner shops here, but multi-million-dollar international corporations with social media pages linked to their websites that haven't been updated for several months, portraying the image they are inactive. The irony is, the opposite situation is usually the case and these companies are actually so busy with their core activities, they just don't have the resources to properly maintain their social media pages.

For businesses looking to get started on social media, the urge is often to dive in and sign up for all the social media accounts going - 'they're free, so we thought we may as well take advantage' is the type of reasoning we hear. However, speaking from experience, nothing could be further from the truth, as success in the social media world again comes down to strategic planning and consistent delivery, always bearing in mind the number one focal point of communications: the target audience. It is much more important to only choose the platforms most suitable for your business and then manage them correctly. The social networks chosen by a corporate law firm should be very different from that of a high street currency exchange - one's target audience is 'other businesses' and particular job functions within organisations; the other is targeting 'anyone who might exchange money'. The priority needs to be the social network where they can best talk to their distinct audiences. It's no surprise the social networks that are less relevant for an organisation's target audience, such as Facebook for a corporate law firm, or the LinkedIn page of a high street currency exchange, fall by the wayside faster. When resources are finite, choose only the most relevant social media networks for your audience and make them better than the competition's pages. You can always add more in future.

The most important thing to consider from the start is the overall objective. It is probably not the best idea to maintain a Twitter account when you can see your competitors get slammed daily by unhappy customers who use it as a complaints platform. On the contrary, you may have ongoing competitions and influencer partnerships planned that are primed to be disseminated through hashtags and will generate organic sharing on an open platform like Twitter.

Another important consideration is content. We recently had a construction company keen for iHC to build and maintain an Instagram account, but they hadn't considered the fact they have limited pictures and videos to post. However, we have a leading architecture firm as a client which is largely comprised of creatives and designers, meaning they have endless ideas, renders and other visually interesting content we can create, such as live sketching, which is has proven to be perfect content for Instagram and ensures their organic engagement levels are impressive.

If you are going it alone and have committed to maintaining your social media platform then you can research various tools that allow you to effectively schedule posting and maintain consistency. Software, such as Buffer and Hootsuite, enables you to share and schedule posts across the major platforms and utilise clever built-in optimisation tools that suggest timings when your posts have the best chance of reaching more of your target audience. They also have useful functions, such as providing suggestions of curated content to share and simple integration with other content-feed tools, such as Feedly and Alltop. Once you get on top of content management, whether or not using any of these simple tools, you can work checking your pages into your daily schedule to respond to queries and comments.

Marketing's ever-enduring 'rule of seven', where a prospect needs to experience the advertiser's message at least seven times before they'll take action, has never had more relevance than in the world of social media marketing. The relationship-based nature of social media means it is easier to maintain positive contact with customers and prospects, developing and sustaining relationships. Many detailed books are written about social media marketing alone and the landscape evolves so quickly. Therefore, I thought it would be valuable to list my top 20 important elements of the discipline, which should help provide some implementable ideas and instil more confidence along the way:

1. Flatter the competition
Some say imitation is the sincerest form of flattery, so don't be afraid to emulate the competition – particularly as you find your feet at the beginning of your social media journey. Analyse how the big brands are working to build and maintain their reputations on social media, as it is likely they have thrown some serious time and resources into it. It is usually a very solid start to research the competition, then simply adopt the best parts of what they do, then you can build confidence and develop your own style.

2. Choose your platforms wisely
It is crucial organisations begin with the networks most relevant for their brand and manage them effectively. It makes sense these social platforms will most likely be

where the target audience is most receptive and, only once they are mastered, is it time to start looking at other social networks. Always consider where your target audience will be and how they would like to receive your messages. LinkedIn, for example, is regarded as ideal for business-to-business communications and the most effective for consultants and service organisations. You can't compare the conservative and highly-targeted options it offers in terms of professional networking with that of sites like Twitter, Facebook or Instagram.

3. Stick to your target audience

It may be nice to feel popular on social media, with so many tiny dopamine hits and ego-boosting engagement levels. However, in business, it is usually more important your activity can be justified by an actual business benefit and your audience targeting is crucial for this. Do not get sucked into promoting to a wider or cheaper audience for increased clicks or follower numbers. Also, sometimes it works well to mix the fun side of life with the serious nature of business, but ensure your social media channels reflect the personality you want your business to portray and do not damage your reputation or credibility. Understand and listen to your audience, creating and discussing content that is important to them and provides them with value.

4. Engagement is key

You wouldn't normally ignore someone who reaches out to you in person so don't ignore them online. This is an opportunity to form a bond with your audience, and building relationships is one of the most important parts of social media marketing success. Make an effort to acknowledge every person who takes the time to reach out to your company. It always impresses me when I see brands on social media communicating and responding efficiently and creatively with customers. You need to consistently publish content and participate in resulting conversations, dedicating time to sharing and talking about content published by others, as the law of reciprocation dictates this is the way others will take the time to share your content.

5. Provide value

Effective social media marketing must always add value, and delivering interesting and relevant content is key to making it a success. If your audience feels like it is being sold to because you begin blatantly promoting your products and services, it will leave. We all know the feeling, so feel free to weave in key messages, but drop the sales pitch.

6. Consider your voice

While getting likes and follows is great, when it comes to building a strong social media presence it is crucial to maintain your brand's true voice. The types of content and conversations you create should always maintain the personality chosen for the brand and operate between the parameters that have been set well in advance. In addition, you might be tempted to share content that will get lots of attention, but if this doesn't tally with your chosen voice, it should be reconsidered.

7. Maintain consistency

Wherever possible try and maintain frequency consistency on your platforms. It is acceptable to adapt your posting strategy, but do try and at least loosely stick to the plan. Whether opting for posting daily on Facebook, or three times daily on Twitter, it can be much easier to maintain an engaged following if you stick to the plan and have discipline and patience with follower and engagement growth. Again, scheduling software can help with this part of the process.

8. Format for each platform
Consider how you plan to deliver the message for each platform, as there are formatting considerations for each. It's not as simple as using the same post for all as, for example, Instagram works best with images, while Twitter requires hashtags and usually tagging of those who might find it interesting. You also need to make the hashtags relevant to the type of search your audience might be carrying out. With LinkedIn, more in-depth posts are acceptable if relevant to the business community, but too much of the fun stuff is usually frowned upon.

9. Remain flexible in your strategy
When embarking upon an integrated communications strategy, the surest thing is that some things will work better than others. Remain vigilant, study inbuilt statistics and monitor what is working and what is not. This should then provide the confidence to make changes in the plan and focus on those tactics that work better. For instance, if you discover four new clients found you through geo-targeted Facebook ads and none have come from the similar Instagram campaign you are running, then consider moving your budget more or even fully across to Facebook. Alternatively, if a pay-per-click sponsored post campaign where $100 on LinkedIn gets 20 clicks from professionals within to your target audience, whereas the same sum gets 100 clicks on Facebook from a much

broader, more random, audience – it is likely another case of quality beats quantity.

10. Activity amplification
One of social media's most potent uses for business is to push out your content to a wider audience. For instance, if you have paid for brand promoters to engage with potential customers and represent your brand at an event or exhibition, get them to take pictures and share content on social feeds - even design a competition to incentivise people to share the content as it happens. Alternatively, if you are presenting at a conference, then have the event's live feed shared on one of your social channels and later promote it to your target audience. If you manage to secure a nice piece of coverage in the top trade website for your business, create a post and advertise this out to your target job titles on LinkedIn. While simple, such tactics are often overlooked when they can amplify the impact of your marketing activities cheaply and effectively.

11. Quality over quantity
Ideally you will be publishing high quality content for your hard-earned audience of quality followers who will share over their own social feeds and blogs, through which you will build an engaged following over time. In addition to this initial benefit, there is the potential for your content to be recycled and posted again over time. It's common for our clients to be contacted by someone who has read some content they enjoyed or found useful that was published several months or even years before.

12. Always consider involving influencers
Spend time finding the online influencers in your market who have quality audiences and are likely to be interested

in your products, services and business. Connect with those people and work to build relationships with them. Even just focus upon finding one and trialling this tactic with them first. Through the process of negotiating with the influencers, if you get on their radar as an authoritative, interesting source of useful information, they might share your content with their own followers, which could put you and your business in front of a huge, relevant new audience.

13. Research software
Have a look around at the various software applications that can be used to pre-schedule posts, saving you time and helping you more efficiently manage your various social media channels. For example, Hootsuite is a popular choice for organisations and we use this for clients. However, it is not cheap for small businesses, with some functions that wouldn't be required by all, but there are many alternative options out there to fit all budgets and requirements. Empower your trusted team to respond quickly to customer questions on important social channels like Facebook, Twitter and Instagram and keep it authentic – rather than a pre-approved sheet of robotic answers.

14. Scan the stats
Take the time to learn what the stats on your social media channels actually mean. At first glance the reports may look daunting, but an hour of your time spent learning and understanding the graphs and figures is all it should take to master it. Particularly if you are spending an advertising budget, you should be monitoring the success of each campaign and comparing engagement between the actions and content you are creating. Through learning

more about your audience, what makes them tick and gives posts the most traction, you can fine-tune your deliverables and really maximise the effectiveness of your channels.

15. Track what is trending

Take advantage of newsjacking – jumping on the back of the biggest news stories, or predicting them before they happen. Own the industry hot topics and become a thought leader through your channels. Twitter can be a great platform for this, where many regular users will follow and begin to take their news from the feeds of accounts they associate with the topic. For example, if you have a veterinary practice and tweet daily about pets, many users might check out your profile when they are looking for their daily cat or dog news fix.

There are no rules against following whoever your competitors are following and who is following them. We have found this a highly-effective and free way of quickly building a relevant following through reciprocal follows. Following and liking people and brands you are targeting will not only encourage them to follow back, but even if they don't you have now entered their conscious. It is a time-consuming process, but worthwhile and should not only be considered as a tactic at the very beginning - but revisited periodically. In short, be a part of the conversation, involve yourself in the relevant topics and engage the audience you are looking for through consistent, communication. If you can make the social media activities enjoyable for yourself, then it will show in your communications.

16. Stimulate your audience

You don't have to be a graphic designer or video producer to create engaging content. There are a multitude of free or easily affordable apps out there, such as Canva for graphic design and Crello for video, dedicated to creating eye-catching social media content, so try them out.

It can also be powerful to generate a two-way conversation through the use of competitions, quizzes or question and answer sessions, where you can cost-effectively fully engage your audience with your brand and take the relationship to the next level. If targeting a distinct audience, you can even create and promote a free webinar (web-based seminar) for a date in the future using platforms like WebinarJam, where you can work towards a date for 45 minutes of directly-imparting knowledge and engaging with new potential clients, then collecting their details through sign-ups for remarketing purposes.

The ideal situation is where your social audience is generating its own content, which can massively increase traffic and (dwell-time) the amount of time they spend on your online property. Take all categories of popular news channels for example, where there will be an article posted, often with little substance, but it creates a debate in the comments section with thousands of engagements. It may not initially seem all that impressive, but when you consider there may be hundreds of thousands of interactions in what is essentially that news channel's online real estate, you can start to see how it strengthens the brand through awareness and even traffic-based advertising revenue.

17. Images are more powerful

Whether it's a high tempo video clip, impactful picture or imaginative meme, the power of imagery in your social media is universally proven to be more effective than words alone. There are a staggering number of studies from trusted sources claiming to have put a number on how much more effective video is than other forms of communication, such as: 'A picture is worth about 1.8m words' and 'viewers who chose to view video converted at a 400 per cent increase over those who did not'. However, what is for certain is that video has little in the way of competition in terms of engaging us and delivering the highest concentration of messages within the shortest period of time – just right for social media.

Social media clips are difficult to beat, in terms of views, dwell time and absorption. As such it is crucial to build this into your communications strategy or be left behind. At our agency, we had to completely revise our packages to offer shorter video clips, as the previous perception of high video costs were preventing clients from committing to this option. We had to instead create plans for raw footage to be taken on one shoot and then separated into 30 second to one-minute clips in order to cover the video producer's time, while still making the exercise worthwhile for the client in terms of output.

Once you begin using video clips it's important to approach your audience in order to get some meaningful feedback. While leading the marketing team at Sportlobster we created a fun show hosted on our YouTube channel called SportlobsterTV, where we had global sporting celebrities, writers and pundits on our tailor-made permanent set. Our experienced presenter, ex-Norwich City, Spurs and Northern Ireland footballer,

Paul McVeigh, interviewed the personalities over a live hour-long show and most who watched gave feedback that they found it to be enjoyable and engaging. However, through subsequent research we discovered the length of the show meant people would save it to watch when they 'had the time', and then forgot about watching it or just never got around to it. Therefore, after several costly episodes, we changed the show to be filmed in several segments at the same time and aired in small chunks, one topic at a time, rather than all at one time. The engagement figures improved dramatically, while the costs were cut through the creation of more episodes from each filming session. The takeaway from the whole experience has stood our agency in good stead: with social media in general, 'less is often better' and being economical with the time of video production can reduce costs significantly and even improve the impact of the results in the process.

18. Showcase

Don't be afraid to show the good things you are doing or creating in your organisation. if you can impart the essence, personality and people of your organisation, it can give them confidence in your brand through the fact your business is demonstrably dynamic. It doesn't always need to be designed, branded content, as people like to see authentic, raw images, footage and snapshots of the corporate culture from time to time, as it can bring to life the real personality of an operation.

19. Build confidence with adverts

Once happy with your content, the next step is to set aside an advertising budget and ensure you are making the most of your activity in terms of reaching out to a new, targeted audience. When new to social media advertising, it's usually best to test the water with a small budget to start with, analysing the results and adapting the next campaign accordingly, as you become comfortable with the success of the efforts. When using social advertising it is also key to have a clear understanding of your objectives from the start. Are you looking to drive awareness, leads or page follows? Which demographic and locations, or even languages and interests are you targeting? The advertising interfaces on social platforms have become so refined and straightforward that most people could use them. However, the trick is to have a very clear vision of what you want to achieve with the allocated budget before activating the campaign.

20. Restrict your audience
Leading from the previous point, once you decide to advertise on a platform, spend some time familiarising yourself with the available options in order to better refine your targeting. If you feel your target audience is in a specific area, is a certain age group or even appeals more to one sex, then begin as targeted as possible and then loosen the reins if and when you feel this is the correct course of action. If you do not do this, then there is the potential side-effect of the audience that, as a consequence of the advertising, begins to follow your page becoming increasingly irrelevant to your brand. I can't stress this point enough: the concept of 'the more followers, the better' is a false economy, as you may begin to see responses and engagements from an audience that doesn't help to you achieve your business goals. It is easy to buy click-farm followers, which have no engagement because they are not real people; or genuine followers from countries where the cost for acquisition is very low,

which is again a useless audience and can even begin to reflect negatively upon your brand and its sincerity. Once you bring on board this type of useless following, it can be tricky to then get rid of them further down the line. Targeting with social media advertising is improving all the time and it is worth having the patience and investing more to obtain a quality following you can build upon over time.

Influencer marketing

"While influencer marketing is an element that can't be ignored by most organisations where consumers are the target audience, the most important thing is to perform adequate research before any collaborations take place, as quality is infinitely better than quantity in this area of marketing," **Michael Campbell, Head of Corporate Communications, Etihad Airways.**

No longer the edgy, awkward new kid mulling around marketing town, influencer marketing is a powerful addition to the communications mix of most types of organisation, which can propel a brand through the social media clutter.

It was an exciting time when I flew to London in 2013 to play my part in an ambitious project, to act as CMO, building an integrated communications team for sport social network, Sportlobster, which had received millions of dollars in funding to push for its place in social media start-up history.

Through preparing a communications strategy alongside the Sportlobster partners, hiring a mix of permanent and interns, who were recent graduates and keen sports fans, we soon had a sizeable communications team delivering a mix of PR, social media, online advertising, influencer marketing, national broadcast advertising and activations to generate awareness and build the number of users on the platform.

While PR played its part in building awareness and, most significantly, in terms of adding credibility to the platform when seeking subsequent trenches of funding, the real success in terms of volume came from different types of influencer marketing, which we used to drive high numbers to the signup page, then a percentage of those went on to register.

From Sportlobster's official launch in April 2013 it enjoyed a steady rise until the launch of the iPhone app that September, when the meticulously planned and coordinated digital launch activity and subsequent communications efforts boosted its user base from 30,000 to 200,000 up until the end of the same year.

A large proportion of this jump was down to building a team of interns dedicated solely to influencer marketing. They were paid on a commission basis, per signup and some made large sums of money in short period of time through finding powerful sport social media sites and paying them to use posts that would send their huge followers to the Sportlobster page - yes, a lot of it was clickbait. Facebook sites like Troll Football, with over two million *engaged* followers, ended up being temporary goldmines for the interns that brokered the deals that resulted in driving heavy traffic to Sportlobster and many thousands of signups to the site. It was an invigorating experience, seeing the numbers on the screen we installed on the wall shoot up when a post was made on an influential page and it became a healthy competition among the team to find and harness the power of these influencers.

A deal was also brokered with Cristiano Ronaldo's team and his brand came on board as a 'superinfluencer' at the beginning of 2019 he had over 120 million Facebook followers and more than 57 million on Twitter. We worked on a content strategy to be approved by his team for his posting and, with him being among the most influential people globally on social media, the numbers driven to the site quickly drove registrations into the seven figures – considered a 'game changer' for the social network at the time.

This practice of brand endorsement is, of course, nothing new. Celebrities have long been sent products to use or have been invited to events, only now it has evolved to also pay for their content in the form of posts and links. On an altogether smaller scale than the world's most popular sport stars, social media has made a form of 'celebrity' a possibility for anyone willing to dedicate a chunk of their lives to social media activity. Whether liked or not by traditionalists, there are enormous numbers of otherwise normal human beings proven to be talented at engaging their audiences to the topics they focus on with their platforms.

Billions of engaged followers of influencers would rather trust their recommendations on what to buy or wear, where to holiday, what to buy their kids, or even which restaurant to book dinner than other sources. People may be the wiser to traditional advertisements and paid-for endorsements, but a paid-for endorsement on an influencer's page will remain stronger than an advert elsewhere in most circumstances, as there is still an inferred element of selection from the influencer you at least appreciated enough to follow.

Depending upon the product or business you are promoting, working with influencers can be a powerful element of your marketing strategy, but doing it properly is not a simple process. With a lack of any regulation it's important to do your due diligence and research any potential influencer's audience, engagement levels and statistics online.

The best results happen if you determine a clear plan for the influencer before approaching them and your brand should be well-aligned with the influencer's own social equity. Put together a plan of expected post frequency, type of content, hashtags, images and video, then present it to the influencer or influential account. This way, you will be taken more seriously by the influencer from the outset and there will be a strong foundation for the negotiations that will form the agreed deliverables. After all, the best results would be content that resonates highly with the influencer's audience, while delivering the key messages of your brand.

It's important not to forget the smaller influencers. Like all forms of sponsorship, if you can forge a relationship with micro-influencers (2,000 – 100,000 followers) on the way up, human nature dictates you can expect them to look favourably upon your brand in future. If you don't have an adequate budget for paid-for endorsements, spend some time researching accounts your audience is following online and foster the relationship – if it is highly targeted, even a small group of followers of an influencer can rapidly improve your awareness levels.

The potential one-on-one conversation your target audience can have with the influencers you team up with has the potential to take engagement to the next-level. In many cases, enhancing this privileged access through question and answer sessions, whether written or through live streaming, can be an effective way to further enhance engagement levels across most platforms.

As a bonus, the potentially high traffic and pure content-marketing nature of influencer marketing can work wonders for your SEO, particularly if you include the sharing of links to data hosted on your own site. Keeping track of such sources of traffic to your website can help you quantify the success of your influencer activity, so ensure you have performance analysis measures in place.

The best influencer work is carried out as a true partnership with your chosen influencer. Always remember they know their audience best and how to make them tick – they have spent months, if not years watching for and responding to reactions and changes in activity. Therefore, it's important to use their voice at all times – make suggestions, but overall let them suggest the best way to deliver the messaging naturally.

So, you may agree a considerable sum for activity with a macro-influencer, or smaller sums with some micro-influencers, but an important element of influencer marketing to address at this point is, whether or not you are paying for your influencer's activity, it is not time to relax and watch the show. Influencer marketing can indeed be a way to make your brand explode, but the best results always happen if you work in tandem with the influencer to ensure the content is authentic, interesting to the audience, but also useful for your brand. This is an important opportunity, so don't leave it up to the influencer to carry out the work alone, or it will inevitably end up in disappointment and, occasionally, conflict when investments are wasted.

So, to reiterate, at Sportlobster we spent a huge amount of money over a relatively short period of time of several months on almost every marketing channel imaginable, which was a steep and expensive learning curve. From the various channels, spanning: YouTube, Google, social channels, national television, publications, outdoor advertising, activations and celebrity endorsement, to name only a few, the tactic that delivered by far and away the best return on investment was the various forms of influencer marketing.

By engaging with, and usually paying, current and ex-sport stars to use the platform and share their link to Sportlobster across their influentially-sized social media accounts, we could enjoy tracking the successes and failures in terms of website activity and registrations live on the office scoreboard screen. An important lesson learnt while using influencers is the diminishing marginal return of posts can be pronounced if sticking too long with the same influencer. We could pay a few thousand pounds to a well-known ex-English Premiership footballer for a series of posts, but we would see perhaps a few hundred signups from the first time they shared a post, which would fall to tens or a few after a number of posts. We used the famous FIFA YouTube gamer, KSI, who drove thousands to the app and billed handsomely for the work. However, despite the early successes, the numbers dropped dramatically when we repeatedly used him, and we soon realised the source of the most-effective influencers to pay and use were generally new ones. It makes sense when you think about it: the message is going to the same audience and, as much as anything else, it becomes less authentic and more irritating the more a follower sees a clearly paid-for brand on the accounts they follow. This is good news for agencies like ours that deal with influencers, as we need to continue activity, recommending and switching the influencers used in order to reach fresh audiences and make the most of client budgets.

There are exceptions of course, especially when the influencers are so well-followed they become superinfluencers. The numbers following superinfluencers can be so immense that even repetitive messages from the same brand can still generate exceptional interest and drive vast traffic. For instance, take the then-Sportlobster superinfluencer Cristiano Ronaldo: everyone knows his team manages his accounts and they are being paid to share corporate messages, but it makes little difference. The sheer numbers of people being driven from his mega-accounts are astonishing. When this happens there are a whole new set of challenges to be faced by organisations who then must be prepared for huge volumes of web traffic entering their platform at the same time and how to effectively deal with and maximise the use of that valuable 'big data'.

From my experience, the best way to harness the power of influencer marketing for your brand is not to build an ongoing partnership with a chosen influencer, but to build a brilliant short-term campaign with them and then move your attention and budget onto the next influencer. This maximises audience reach, maintains authenticity and keeps the creative juices flowing.

To recap, a few general benefits of using influencer marketing:

Simplicity: you don't need previous experience to test the water with influencer marketing. With some thorough research and planning you can confidently engage an influencer through their social channel and request a collaboration. You can then evaluate the success or failure of your efforts and decide whether to repeat the exercise, try something different, or engage an agency to help with the next effort.

Cost-effectiveness: in stark contrast to other marketing methods, some forms of micro-influencer marketing can cost you no more than a considerable time investment and the cost of sending produce. For example, we promoted international jewellery brand, Lovisa, throughout the Middle East through identifying over 100 key fashion and lifestyle influencers and key media to target. All were contacted directly and asked whether they would like to sample the new collection in return for mentions. Gift bags were created and samples sent for the influencers to use as giveaways, which resulted in priceless features of the product across a huge target audience and ongoing mentions through giveaways to the influencers' audience, at a fraction of the cost of advertising.

Novelty: influencer marketing continues to increase in popularity, but it is still relatively new in the marketing industry. Therefore, it remains the case for many businesses that getting involved earlier than competitions could leave competitors standing before *they* get their influencer game into gear. Also, like anything fairly new, you have more opportunity to do something truly unique and creative before someone else thinks of it.

Before you begin contacting all your target influencers, take a few minutes to go through my ten influencer marketing considerations:

1. Strategy
Do the research, look at your competitors, revisit your objectives, set your budget and then evaluate a set of influencer options, putting it down in writing before you do anything further. While this skeleton strategy should remain flexible and, as such, is unlikely to be the end-result, it will help you set parameters and hold you back from getting carried away with actions that are outside your current means. Keep in mind influencers can also be talented sales people and the successful ones are regularly negotiating deals and refining their upsell tactics.

Your preparedness should earn you respect from the influencer further down the line, and you will always be in a stronger position if you go in with the offer and what you want in return than if you approach a negotiation looking in any way naive. For example, when launching the

Sportlobster app, our influencer marketing team approach started with a huge target list on the wall of the sporting celebrities, fan accounts and other related networks and what we would offer them to all 'chatter' about the app on the day we launched it - using ex-footballer, Michael Owen, himself a sporting influencer, as the focal point of the combined online PR, social media and influencer launch. We approached each influencer with an offer, and while there was a certain amount of wiggle-room, if it wasn't enough for them, we moved on. Very few said they didn't want to get involved because they considered our offer too meagre for their time. The result was a coordinated explosion of information about the app launch across social media, which achieved our target of our audience not being able to avoid the news. Most sports fans knew there was a new sport social network launched and had the app download link in their feeds, whether they liked it or not. As a strategic decision all this was executed for a fraction of the cost of a physical launch event, which is unlikely to have translated into app downloads or anything like the awareness levels we generated among the target audience of young sports fans.

As part of your strategy, it is advisable to set measurable, realistic overall goals for the campaign, which can then later be negotiated and agreed with the influencers themselves, helping with motivation, expectation-synergy and could even be built into eventual remuneration or bonus packages.

2. Budget
Decide upon your campaign's *initial* influencer budget and stick to it. How much you will allocate to your influencer

marketing budget is less straightforward than other forms of marketing. However, we recommend starting with a sum that is a minimum to deliver noticeable results and then, once confidence builds and results are delivered, it is easier to gradually increase the budget, perhaps by diverting funds from other forms of marketing that are proving less cost-effective.

Testing the water with a single-influencer campaign is easy to gauge through the usual analytics, such as Google Analytics, but if you are using a number of influencers, it is still possible to monitor the success of the campaign, breaking it down per-influencer using tracking links from providers such as Bitly and ClickMeter. At Sportlobster we not only incentivised some influencers for every app download that happened as a result of the links they posted, but we also incentivised our influencer marketing executives who, through earning up to 50p per download, made thousands of pounds per week when they found influencers who drove large volumes of downloads.

However, the caveat here is, some influencers were driving huge volumes of app downloads, but then those downloading were not registering, so it transpired we were paying a lot of money for results that weren't achieving the final goal. Therefore, we had to bring down our payments per click and change the payment system to focus upon registrations, ensuring we stuck to our budget. With influencer marketing it's crucial to remain flexible, but always maintain financial controls, as things can change or accelerate rapidly, such is the fluid nature of social networking.

3. Tools

We have already mentioned link trackers, which are a must when running influencer marketing campaigns. However, you should also become an expert on Google Analytics and using it to analyse the activity and journey the hard-earned traffic to your site is taking. There are also myriad global influencer research platforms to help you find, choose and engage with influencers, such as Iconosquare and Socialbakers, with most having a free trial period, so you can experiment with a few, then settle on the one you find easiest to use.

4. Mixing

Not everyone can afford to pay for influencers or have the brand reputation clout to strike a bargaining deal with influencers who have a six-figure following, never mind a superinfluencer, such as a Kardashian, Ronaldo, Messi, or a chart-topping music star. However, don't be disheartened, as a great deal can be accomplished with a mix of influencers of different sizes. The most important element is that they have to genuinely hold your target audience. For example, if you are selling a sports supplement in only one city and you have a small budget, the budget could well be better spent working with ten well-followed local physical trainers and respected bodybuilders or fitness models, rather than a globally-famous celebrity influencer in the fitness space, such as Kayla Itsines, who can sell out stadium tours in hours and has over ten million Instagram followers.

And remember one of the most important elements of influencer marketing: follower count is often irrelevant - it's all about the engagement of the following and the fit of their target audience to your objectives. Often smaller influencers have a better niche audience for your brand.

5. Creativity

Wherever possible, harness the creativity of the influencers you are working with, as it is their content that attracted their audience in the first place. Again, authenticity is key, and it is only through content that is driven by the influencer will the end result look genuine - and probably truly interesting. The clever input from your side is to mix your brand into the content in a way that is effective, *but subtle*. The use of product placement can often be the best form of adding your commercial ingredients into the creative mix, when the product is an integral part of the plausible story. An example could be promoting key properties for a holiday home booking app by offering them to celebrities, then sending a video crew to make a fantastic one-minute clip that can then be pushed out and promoted on the app's social channels, plus the celebrity's channels and used across marketing collaterals. Or ambitious photographers, who will offer their services to celebrities for a mention in return for working with them on a free family shoot, or inventing another scenario where they can generate some fantastic shots appropriate for the snapper's portfolio. Such is the amount of business that can be generated from influential social media endorsements that sometimes it can only take a few posts by the right influencer and the returns for this free investment can mean a reservations book filled up for weeks - that's before even taking into account the substantial residual legacy kudos.

However always beware most audiences do not like to feel they are being force-fed messages, so err on the side of creativity-over-commercialism and you are likely to improve the results. Work closely with the influencer and help provide high-quality but authentic, rich visual content to maximise the impact the influencer can deliver.

6. Quality
As with most things related to marketing a business, brand, product or service - quality beats quantity. Unless you have an endless budget, it is always of primary importance you are hitting your target audience with your messages every time. Influencer marketing is no different. Dig deeper into the audience of the influencer you are targeting, check their engagement levels, who is responding to posts and where they come from.

Paid-for tools like Iconosquare or Social Blade can give decent insights into page follower demographics, but also don't be shy to ask the influencer to share their analytics for a period relevant to your proposed campaign. In the interests of true partnership and transparency, if someone has an issue with sharing such information, then there might be something to hide.

Generally referred to as 'vanity metrics', we have had plenty clients ask us to buy them 20,000 followers so their operation looks bigger than it is. It's not something we have ever wanted to get involved in or connected to, because it causes irreversible future issues with demographics and engagement. However, many have gone ahead and organised it themselves - purchasing followers from click-farms. Highly engaged, authentic accounts on any platform - not just Instagram - can outperform suspect accounts with ten times their following, so be very wary of this.

Also bear in mind some accounts that have an engaged target audience still might not be receptive to your brand messages. For example, an account run by an attractive bikini model with millions of followers might seem the ideal platform to get messages out about your miraculous new skin cream, then when you dig deeper you discover a huge percentage of her following is actually enamoured men.

7. Investigation

Closely following on from points made in number six, not only should you perform due diligence on the influencer social media account, but you need to spend some time researching the past of the person or people behind the page. The last thing you want to do is sign a contract for a campaign, then discover your new brand ambassador has a murky or controversial past, or potentially damaging beliefs you could have found if you had trawled through Google long enough.

8. Negotiation

The figures and projections for the influencer marketing industry vary, but most are agreed the industry is heading into the billions of dollars annually. The subjective, and often personal, nature of influencer marketing makes pricing in particular chaotic and highly variable. It can be an unnerving step into the unknown negotiating with an influencer, particularly when you might not be able to apportion a financially-meaningful figure to the results.

We see all imaginations of fanciful rate cards flying into our office email every week, from micro to macro influencers and their agents, looking for huge sums per post or series of posts. Some are looking for US$500 to do 'something' together, right up to the better-known options, who are asking for six figures for the pleasure of working together. However, be prepared to counter offer with something that works for your business. For example, some of the biggest influencers we have worked with in the past have agreed to an ongoing relationship in exchange for some brand equity, so keep this type of non-cash offer in mind if you are trying to keep your marketing expenditure down and have identified a potentially special influencer partnership.

We have rarely found influencers unwilling to listen to a pitch offer with a brand's terms - particularly if the brand is of particular interest to the influencer's target audience. We have had great success with products for giveaway to an influencer's audience with little or no additional payment, but ensure you have researched their content and audience before pitching to them.

9. Integration
The best campaigns are nearly always approached in holistic way. Don't plough all your efforts and budget into your influencer campaign at the expense of your other marketing channels. Real power can be generated through a complementary strategy that amplifies the work you are doing in your influencer marketing. You can use PR, social media marketing, online advertising, events and other methods to push the content and messages out to a much larger audience and encourage organic curiosity and momentum. This might include using the same campaign hashtag and creative throughout everything, retaining ownership of the ongoing campaign for long after the influencer's input has ended.

10. Analysis

As with many areas of marketing, measuring the financial success of an influencer marketing campaign remains a challenge, as it is difficult to meaningfully measure the impact of brand awareness. However, if making a considerable investment, it is important to set key performance indicators (KPIs) for each campaign.

The number of interactions on a post will rarely be a measure of success, so instead carefully analyse link performance and traffic behaviour in order to see which influencer posts were successful, what the outcomes were and identify the behaviour of those who have been attracted through the activities. Too often overlooked, or not enforced stringently enough by clients, it is imperative the sources of leads and sales are recorded during marketing campaigns. Each influencer and every post should have its own link-tracking in place and someone should be assigned to generate a report on the activity to evaluate and, in an ideal world, potentially reward the influencer based upon a part performance-related agreement.

You should have set KPIs relevant to your business before beginning the campaign, such as: web traffic, enquiries, impressions, interactions, leads, calls or followers, putting the same amount of effort into these elements as you would with any other marketing activity. In addition, proper analysis will help you identify what worked best and tweak your campaign for the better the next time.

Four influencer marketing ideas that have a proven track record of success:

Piggybacking: create content related to your product or service that makes the most of trending news or seasonal topics, for example: world health days, major sporting or entertainment occasions, holidays, celebrations and seasons.

Promotions: create a competition and prize or conceive an offer for a limited time, which encourages the audience to get involved. This can be particularly effective if it encourages production of shareable user-generated content, for example: users need to post and share a picture or video to enter.

Experiences: heavily used by the tourism and hospitality industries, as it is relatively cheap for them to offer trips and stays for locations when the places are vacant. Businesses in this sector can benefit from huge exposure through impressions and engagement as influencers authentically depict their journey and experiences.

Causes: the heady mix of influencers and a shared cause can reap rewards through a combination of trust and emotion. This can generate serious engagement if the messages strike a chord with the target audience. For example: home appliances brand, Beko, recently raised over a million euros for UNICEF to help fight child obesity, donating a euro to the charity for each post shared using the hashtag #EatLikeAPro, capitalising on its sponsorship of Barcelona FC and connecting the brand to healthy eating habits and lifestyle through the content produced by influencers. Influencers were asked to produce three pieces of content and the hashtag was promoted heavily around the El Clásico match between Barcelona FC and rivals Real Madrid. The brand leveraged its sponsorship of the team and generated more than three million impressions on Instagram alone through the target-relevant family-themed posts created by influencers.

Online advertising

"It's difficult to understand why some businesses don't use online advertising, when it's so clear it could improve their income almost immediately. Test the water, then increase the budget if and when you begin seeing the results. It could hardly be any simpler," **Jon Kettle, owner, Taxicode.**

The number of successful businesses we encounter as an agency that do not have any level of paid online advertising in place is astonishing. For many types of organisation, it is the cheapest, most manageable and scalable source of sales, leads and traffic available. While some smaller businesses might think they don't have a chance of cost-effectively competing with big-budget competitors on pay-per-click (PPC) Google ads, the world's number one advertising platform has ensured no one should be discouraged from signing up and sending them some money to promote their business, by putting algorithms in place to ensure even modest budgets can generate some clicks.

AdWords may well be relatively user-friendly and accessible to all budgets, but it is also a vast, ever-changing and complicated platform to master, which is the reason agencies such as ours exist. However, it is also structured so anyone can test the water and create a basic advert that should almost immediately drive traffic to a web page. However, if you do take the plunge and have a go at starting your own AdWords campaign, you should be prepared to log in on a daily basis, check the various key metrics and ensure your budget isn't being sucked into a black hole. There's no recourse if your month's budget for your second-hand car dealership goes on people randomly checking out antique car pictures, just because you haven't set your negative keywords up sufficiently. A common irritator for those new to AdWords is paying for clicks by people looking for jobs, which can simply be covered with your ever-expanding negative keywords list. Google gets paid regardless. However, the more time you spend on your account, learning the nuances, testing new keywords and campaigns and understanding your audience, the more impressive the returns.

Before you begin AdWords, it's important you have your website and landing pages in order. If you create a separate landing page for each product or service, it will help in several ways, such as improving your quality score, conversion rate, reduce your cost per click and improve your click-through rate. And, as with most things Google does, intuitively it makes sense. The customer journey is going to be simpler if they are landing on exactly the right page as the item or information they clicked an advert to see. How many times have you clicked an advert online, only to be taken to a page that's either not what you want or then too complicated or poorly laid out to find what exactly you are looking for? Often, you will simply click 'back' and go find another more useful link to what you are looking for - increasing the advertiser's bounce rate and wasting their budget. The landing pages you are driving traffic to are crucial and should include keywords that mirror those of the adverts and exactly describe your product and service. You should also always have your main keywords in the landing page URL. Stay away from waffle and focus on keywords that your customers would be searching for and differentiate your product or service from others.

Before setting up your initial AdWords campaign set some time aside alone or with your team and consider the keywords people will search for to find your company, services and products. These should be prevalent throughout your website, AdWords campaign and any other online content you invest time in. The more consistency in your messaging over a prolonged period of time, the easier Google can connect you with your target audience, helping optimise your search ranking against competitors.

Once you have an initial set of preferred keywords in place for each Ad group, Google's automated Keyword Planner will automatically suggest other related popular keywords and even show the number of searches for those keywords, to help you along the way. The goal of each landing pages can vary significantly with the company, product or service, but there should always *be* a goal. This might be to fill out a form, hit the call button, download a brochure, subscribe to a blog, or even click to buy a product, but whatever the goal is should be clear and easy to find. In terms of content, there should be a clear call to action; clean and not cluttered and usually an attractive image or eye-catching piece of content, such as a video clip or portfolio scroller.

Establishing Google Analytics is straightforward and should be done as soon as possible, so you can begin understanding your traffic better, viewing its behaviour and journey when arriving on your website, refining your AdWords campaign to maximise results from the spend. This will require a token to be added to your website, in order for Google can access the back-end, so follow the setup instructions in Google Analytics and, if you can't manage first time, search for a step-by-step guide on YouTube.

Start small with your budget, erring on the side of caution. Use 'exact match' types to begin with so there are fewer wasted clicks. Then you can progressively grow your account, expand your campaign budget and test bidding strategies for each ad group connected to each landing page. You should build confidence and become increasingly adept at attracting the right traffic, and you should begin to see an increasing number of worthwhile leads.

As mentioned, there are few newcomers to AdWords who haven't experienced some budget sucked away through useless clicks because the keywords had not been set up correctly. Therefore, particularly in the beginning, regularly check the keyword search terms. For example, our agency also provides photography services, therefore 'photography' was at one point a solitary keyword, which meant hundreds of people who were looking for all sorts of random pictures were clicking on the advert and we lost hundreds of dollars over a weekend. Don't underestimate how many people will click ads and within a short period of time, particularly if the keywords are broad and vague. Start with keywords as specific as possible, such as 'best doctors in Abu Dhabi' or 'wedding photographer in Edinburgh', then broaden it out and add variations as you go along – build it up over time.

You must decide carefully the locations, devices, demographics and timings for which you would like your ads to run. Which brings us to another important point: if you have set up AdWords to drive calls to your office 24/7 and there is only someone there to answer the phone between 9-6pm, five days a week, then it is likely a waste of budget and could also be off-putting for your potential customer.

Set a monthly budget, break it down to a daily budget and then keenly watch, investigate and learn how your money is being spent and where to adapt, pause, reduce and increase. Test different adverts for each Ad group and a minimum of three ad variations for each Ad group is recommended - then Google itself will pick what it considers to be the most effective for each query. Another tip is: if you are trying something new, then always pause rather than delete the old Campaign, Ad group or Ad, when you create the new one, as this way you can compare results rather than lose the data for ads you have already paid for.

Once you have determined your maximum bid, the work you have done so far and the resulting quality score will go some way to determining your ad positioning for keyword searches, after taking into account competitor bids. You do not need to be the first advert on the page in order to be successful. In fact, many prefer to be third because it is cheaper and places you one place above the number one organic result. If the budget you are comfortable with isn't even in the top three, then it's okay as it is best to be patient and play it safe somewhere on the first page until the results start showing.

In most types of business, you should consider establishing contact forms for each landing page, perhaps an automated chatbot to answer enquiries, such as Zopim, or a pop-up like Optinmonster to grab the paid for traffic that has come to your page and is leaving without taking any action and other data collection and remarketing plugins for your site, such as subscribers.com.

We have so far covered pay-per click (PPC), which is primarily text and by far the simplest and most commonly used form of paid advertising - an excellent platform to test the water with online advertising. Results are often quick and impressive, so be prepared to get 'hooked' and soon expand your time and financial resources committed on this form of promoting your business.

Display advertising is the next stage to consider, where you can begin campaigns that show banner ads on Google affiliate sites. This form of advertising can be highly effective, particularly with the added benefit of more visual brand awareness - plus it is often cheaper per-click than the PPC alternative. However, it can also be more complicated to set up, should be designed properly to remain on-brand and usually has lower sales conversions than the text PPC alternative. Put simply: people browsing websites and viewing network display adverts are not actively looking to buy a product or service, or they would be using the search network.

Once everything is in place, you can spend some time establishing remarketing, which will allow you to maximise your conversion rate with potential customers who have viewed your wares, but not yet taken the plunge. Like an angler's fly repeatedly being passed across a salmon's nose until it finally snaps and takes the bait, remarketing will show your ads to people who have previously shown interest. With varying statistics on remarketing claiming potential customers who see retargeted ads are as much as 70 per cent more likely to convert, this tactic undoubtedly yields high conversion rates and can be an effective way to make the most of more modest budgets. It is relatively straightforward to activate remarketing in your AdWords setup and there are plenty online tutorials to help you along the process. Probably the most common form of remarketing people experience is when online shopping. When we abandon our carts, through remarketing our social and Google feeds begin aggressively reminding us of the products we nearly bought, attempting to drive us back to the sale. Some research on this has shown over three times as many people are likely to return to their abandoned shopping cart if remarketing is used to attract them there.

The myriad ways marketing can help promote your business in terms of brand awareness and sales or lead generation is unarguable. However, where many marketing tactics fall down in terms of measurability, AdWords is extremely successful and advanced in this regard. It has precise targeting, impressively detailed metrics and is somewhat user-friendly, considering the complexity of the platform. The complete control over budgets and access to effective technologies, such as remarketing and user-friendly display options, all within what is effectively a monopolistic search engine - so you know most of your customers will *be* there - make it difficult to ignore as part of your marketing mix.

While it is often the best first port of call as a promotional tool to make sales, AdWords is not the only form of online advertising out there, so consider the other options for your business. For example, online directories can be another simple and cost-effective source of paid leads and some offer unpaid options to test the water. Perform Google searches for your company's products or services as if you were a customer and as you scroll pages you will find directory listings. Ensure you are listed on all of the free options, as over time they should drive some leads to your page, despite the fact you will be listed lower than the paid-for alternatives. Once you have registered, most will periodically mail you with how many clicks they have sent to your site, or you can go and discover this information by logging in to the directory.

Within a few days of setting up Google Analytics, you can then also track where your traffic is coming to your website from. We often find useful directories for clients through analysing traffic sources in their Google Analytics, which gives us the confidence to purchase a paid listing and we then compare the difference in results. If a directory is particularly successful and you then trial a paid ad, which usually brings your listing to the top of their page, then you can compare the cost versus traffic or leads against that of AdWords. Once you have delved deeper into conversions, you can put a figure on the value of AdWords against other paid campaigns, such as directories or other onsite ads within specific sites of interest to your target audience.

Neo-SEO

"It is crucial your company's website is fit-for-purpose according to the current requirements of Google and optimised to perform the best it possibly can on search engines. There are few things more valuable to a business than the leads that can be generated and received through carefully prepared landing pages. We have converted large contracts over recent years through our ongoing work in this area. Anyone promoting their business must take advantage of the various platforms in place to improve their performance on Google and ensure both on-page keywords and content marketing maximise the amount of traffic generated - and its quality," Jim Muldoon, MD, Losberger De Boer.

I was diagnosed with having an intuitive management style by one of those 'leadership consultants' several years ago. Being an 'Intuitor' is apparently not as bad as it sounds, as they merely require the freedom to do things their own way, are perennially curious and easily inspired, which are some traits that can apparently be successful in business. From experience and the information at hand, intuitively it makes sense to me traditional search engine optimisation (SEO) is not *dead*, as many experts claim, but it is definitely a shadow if its former self - and this tallies with our agency experience over recent years.

The world of SEO has become a particularly controversial one in the wider marketing conversation. The very nature of traditional SEO's battle with Google makes the discipline so capricious and the constant changes fall heavily to Google's benefit. It is simply extremely difficult to beat a quasi-monopoly, which has all the budget and technological talent to ensure it remains the clear leader and stays ahead of the SEO marketing industry's ongoing efforts to manipulate and expose loopholes in Google's system. The good news is many of these ongoing changes provide a clearer path for everyone to deliver simple SEO steps that really work for your business.

In 2015 we hired a traditional SEO agency - a large, fast-growing outfit with lots of impressive brands already on board - to handle our own agency's SEO on retainer for several months as a test before potentially white-labelling for clients. This experience resulted in some serious issues arising in our website when the SEO firm was granted access to optimise its backend for search. Our landing page rankings actually fell over the period and every monthly report seemed like it was trying to flummox us with reams of pages of technical jargon we didn't have immediate time to get around to analyse. Then when we did dig deeper into the results, many questions were raised and issues required resolving, such as poor English being inserted into our meta tags. The SEO agency always seemed to provide well-rehearsed answers that sounded like agency excuses to well-versed agency ears. This experience and subsequent encounters with SEO agencies have shaped our outlook on SEO. It seems there are many

SEO companies out there pedalling an easily-scalable monthly package of traditional SEO tactics where they are using low-cost, third-world SEO staff to create articles stuffed with keywords and links and run them through a collection of obscure paid-for, third-party websites in order to, in theory, move up the rankings. While they are clearly doing very well from providing this type of service - which starts from only a few hundred dollars a month as a monthly retainer - I don't believe it is the best avenue to begin building SEO for your business.

Our agency's subsequent reluctance to employ this type of traditional SEO 'package' has certainly been to our financial detriment, as I am certain we have lost new business pitches where the marketing director has sat there cradling his SEO budget and raising an eyebrow at our alternative standpoint and tactics. Google has been consistently investing boundless resources to ensure it minimises abrasion of its advertising income due to traditional SEO practices 'cheating the system'. As an agency, we prefer to focus our efforts upon ensuring our clients produce content that is more relevant to those searching and is therefore of greater use to Google. Google and other third-party developers have devised user-friendly platforms where we can improve web rankings and traffic - but on Google's terms. We call our take on the discipline 'neo-SEO' a new outlook on search optimisation, rather than the dark arts of the past. Without getting too technical, this section will focus on some elements of neo-SEO I believe to be the best practical foundations for ensuring your business is well optimised in terms of search. Get these foundations right first, then as you learn more, make decisions about potentially digging down deeper into SEO and traffic generation and hiring an outside party for extra assistance.

With Google handling trillions of searches every year and a significant proportion of these - some report as high as half - having local intentions, the smart place to begin your neo-SEO is through Google My Business (GMB). It has been designed with non-marketing experts in mind, so is relatively simple to learn and always improving, so you should master this platform and its various elements in relation to your business activities. Crucial to ensuring you command as much first page Google real estate as possible, with simple interfaces to push out searchable content and make your business location prominent on Google Maps, GMB plays a major part in how your audience finds you online. Put some focused hours in up-front, then dip into it at least on a weekly basis. Download the app to your smartphone, keep track of changes and improvements and own this fantastic resource for promoting your business, which can make a real difference to your search engine performance, traffic and, ultimately, bottom line.

Taking the time to complete your GMB profile as thoroughly as possible will pay back your time investment many times over and help potentially thousands on the journey to your business. There are many excellent YouTube guides and articles already out there to follow if you ever become stuck. Nevertheless, I've put together a list of pointers that could really help you make the most of your listing, as follows:

Before going through the GMB process, it is useful to first search for your company's services on Google's search engine. You should see listings from competitors in your city, so take note of what you would like to copy and elements you would adapt and improve for your own listing. Perform the same searches in Google Maps and take notes in advance for what you are looking to achieve.

Take care in choosing your main category selection, which will play a bigger part in searches and in future rankings, so this needs to be your core business and you can then add additional categories, if applicable and, of course, your company provides these products or services. Again, this is not a case of 'the more the better', so focus only on your key areas, as stuffing in services that don't really represent your business will only succeed in misrepresentation, with mass-irritation a potential consequence.

Use all the characters in your business description. However, only a third show up before they get cut off in the Knowledge Panel, so ensure you put the most important information and keywords towards the front of the description. Honesty is the best policy. You are not trying to trick Google like other traditional SEO methods - you must instead maintain focus on making the experience as efficient as possible for the customer.

You should use your actual real-world business name, not with your location tagged on, and select your real location. If you have a virtual business then think twice about adding it if no one can actually visit you, and certainly don't mark it as being 'open'. Let's say the potential customer found your virtual office listing, sees it is open, so drives across the city to find nothing there - they will dislike your business and probably report as much with one star in your reviews section.

As with AdWords, use your actual working hours, because another common irritator is when companies list themselves as a 24-hour operation, perhaps not wanting to lose out on business leads, then are uncontactable within certain hours. This can turn a person off your organisation due to the fact their first experience has been a failure. Listed hours are better to be set as when your physical office is open and the listed contact details are in operation. You can even add 'special hours' in, if you have an office holiday on a certain day, such as Christmas or Eid, so potential customers are made aware in advance. Provide the website that contains your actual business location, not a social platform, and if you have multiple office locations, create a local page for each.

GMB Posts
A must for any business, the rise of GMB Posts has been an important addition to our agency's communications arsenal, and the additional awareness it creates and traffic it generates makes very good reading for clients in our monthly reports. The posts allow you to engage directly with your target audience on Google search, providing more 'ever-welcome' first page real estate. It is simple to share content from all the planned monthly communications activity - from news to case studies, tips, events and offers. Posts expire every week and you are then conveniently reminded by Google via email to add another. Again, only the first few sentences show up in your Knowledge Panel, so ensure the start of each post holds the most important messages. You can have a number of live posts at once and all should have an accompanying image or video clip, but you are better to post consistently, rather than adding ten at a time every

six months. In almost all situations you should add a call-to-action on posts, from 'Book', to 'Call' or 'Order Online', depending upon which is most relevant for your business. For those who don't have the time to host their own content on their website, or pay an agency to do so, this can even act as a type of blog that is connected to search and can help increase lead generation.

GMB Reviews
Having more good reviews of your organisation than your competitors is a key differentiator and can improve your lead generation. Consider if you are searching for a service and Google returns five listings but one has double the reviews, with a higher rating. Which listing are you more likely to click on? Google also rewards businesses for having reviews by ranking them higher against competitors on search. Therefore, this is a crucial area of neo-SEO all too often ignored, where you can quickly optimise your search by following some simple steps.

It is important to respond to both negative and positive reviews and Google has again helped us with this by emailing a link every time we receive a review in order to click and reply. Remember potential customers will also read your feedback, so don't be shy about adding more details about what was delivered and the USPs in there.

You can also apply to remove a review you feel is unjust or fake, but you will have to furnish Google with proof and a compelling argument for taking this action. However, don't worry when you get your first review below five stars, as it can look less than authentic when a company has only five-star reviews. The golden star beside your company's link, showing you indeed have reviews, already sets it ahead of those with none.

Be proactive about getting reviews from happy customers. We regularly send a personalised message by email or WhatsApp from an edited template, with a direct link to the review section, asking our customers to click and review. Always check the link on an incognito window or a colleague's computer, to ensure it works as a direct link before sending to the customer as, from experience, people usually don't like to perform more than one click to find the correct review page.

GMB Uploads - Photos, Video, 360° Interactive Tour
Before taking the plunge and choosing to contact your business instead of your competitor, potential customers want to know what your business is, where it is located exactly, how it looks and as many other details as possible. If you are proud of your business location, want to demonstrate its activities and showcase its products and services in order to attract more custom, it is easy to upload photos, video, and even content like a 360° interactive tour, to stand out from the competition.

We have seen impressive monthly traction from GMB listings across many industry types, with some regularly attracting thousands of views a month simply through us uploading images along the way as we create them, whether they be profile shots, event images or news photography. There is a healthy appetite for this content and it helps quickly build trust in your brand. As long as the content is reflective of your company, there are no real limitations to what you can upload, so have some fun with it and get into the habit of uploading regularly, even if you must schedule it weekly or monthly. According to Google My Business, businesses with photos get 40 per cent more requests for directions and the upload interface is easy, so there is really no excuse.

With video uploads, you already have more freedom to explain your business and they can work incredibly well for visually-selling things like destinations, attractions or hospitality venues. However, if you run an accountancy firm, then ten people in an office working on spreadsheets is unlikely to have new clients queueing at the reception. If you want to be extra-creative, then add a welcome video, where you can say something about the company and mention a few reasons why anyone should choose your business over others. Keep it short, usually 30 seconds is most impactful for this type of clip. If the way your business looks is a main selling point, such as a luxury hotel or spa, then investing in a 360° interactive tour is a sensible option, as it will show off your offering to the fullest.

Once you're already on top of the basic listing, take it a step further by adding advanced information throughout the platform wherever relevant. Take advantage of any additional gadgets that are provided for your chosen type of business, such as adding product prices, a booking button or a text messaging facility. Depending on your business and services, GMB will provide different options in order to optimise the user experience, so make the most of the options you have at your disposal, because you can be sure your competitors will.

Website optimisation

While most new sites are pretty well optimised through the advanced technologies existing in web development favourites like WordPress, Wix and Squarespace, if you have an old site, it might to be time to speak to an agency or trusted developer and have them check it for optimisation. Older websites that don't respond well to mobile device usage and aren't built with current search engine algorithms in mind are often only good for the scrapheap. With so many new clients we have taken on in recent years to market their businesses, we have had to take a step back and first build a new website before carrying out any communications activity. On-site optimisation is a collection of tactics, most of which are simple to implement and geared toward making your website more visible and indexable for search engines. These tactics include actions such as: optimising your titles, keywords and meta descriptions to include more of your business' main details, core services, and USPs; ensuring your site's code is clean and minimal and provides ample, relevant content on every page. It also covers elements such as page load speed and mobile compatibility, combining many elements to ensure your website is deemed to be providing a positive user experience by Google.

Get your website up to scratch and revisit it regularly in order to update and tweak. Your website's relevance is a measure of how appropriate your content is for an incoming query and can be easily adapted with keyword selection and content creation. You need to work on your site to build its authority, which is how trustworthy Google views your site to be. Your site authority should improve over time as your content improves and you generate inbound links and brand mentions through the various integrated communications activities you will undertake. Consider tools that might be relevant for your business in terms of collecting information from those that visit your site and adding them to your funnel, while improving their experience along the way. This might be data capture pop-ups; chatbots that answer while there's no one working; automated browser remarketing software or a click magnet, where you are offering a free promotion, such as a downloadable guide or a competition entry in exchange for their data. A big difference can be made to your website's lead generation success by simply adding clickable links and one-click call buttons for mobile phones. You would be amazed at the number of companies out there - even marketing agencies themselves - where you still have to copy and paste a phone number from a site to call it, which is fidgety and many people would rather just click onto the next website than bother with the process.

Voice
One of the hottest topics in neo-SEO is voice search, which is widely regarded among many experts as the fastest growing type of search. As technology improves and voice search devices, such as Google's Assistant or Amazon's Alexa, become increasingly robust and sensitive, the speed and convenience of voice search is undeniable, as it takes its place as part of the Internet of Things within an increasing number of offices and homes.

Voice search as a tool is only going to increase in popularity, so a strategy for utilising it should be included in any website upgrades. In general, when it comes to search, the conversational way we would search in a spoken form should be taken into account when making future decisions. Also, where traditional SEO was about getting onto the first page of Google search, voice search is much more competitive, as it is the first featured snippet displayed above the first organic result - there can only be one winner. I can see I am now getting into the technical aspects of this, which is perhaps where to end, as there are hundreds of free in-depth, colourful step-by-step guides to optimising for voice search. The main point is: it's already something many companies need to look at in terms of their search optimisation and future website upgrades.

It's also important to note, while all businesses *should* consider voice search, its use will be much more common with certain types of organisations. For example, voice search lends itself to specific searches such as 'What is the nearest cinema?', rather than, 'Who are the top marketing agencies in Rio?' Therefore, if your business fits into the former category, it is even more important you learn about voice search and ensure your company is Alexa's new 'best friend forever'.

External content marketing
One of trickier elements of SEO is content marketing for external websites or guest posting, which traditional SEO marketers would call link-building. If we look back to when Google appeared on the scene in the late nineties, linking was one of its key differentiators that landed killer blows on the many other popular search engines, such as AltaVista and Ask Jeeves, as it used external links to evaluate the quality of web pages through its PageRank algorithm, which it still uses to this day. Rather like the way citations work in academia, lots of pages pointing to a page simply indicates that page is of a higher quality than

another; while links from pages ranked with high authority are an even stronger indicator of quality.

Link-building has since been a major component of SEO and link builders would ask other website owners to link to their site, usually with a reciprocal link offered in return - we've all received the emails. Fast forward to today's neo-SEO era and link-building has become a much more difficult task, which relies upon creating content worthy enough for other sites to use and this is the way links are more likely to be built. Once again Google is forcing all its users to provide more value to its search engine and for each other, which is another clever move that is enriching our online experience and forcing people like us to try harder and create content.

The idea of having to 'put yourself out there' is a big turn off for many, but Google is big on this and the rewards can be impressive in terms of optimising your site. The goal is to create content on external websites, building your company, and often your personal brand at the same time, through getting the external sites to link back to your site as a reward. However, capable modern content marketers know the tactic isn't about firing your links off to as many external pages as possible and hoping for success. It is about creating relevant, valuable content for target websites that people want to read, including links that appear naturally within that content. If the hosting websites are well ranked, these links will, over time, boost your search relevance because you are adding value to users and, of course, the Google experience.

So, there you have it, neo-SEO encompasses much more than just forcing backlinks, stuffing keywords, getting your website optimised and battling those pesky Google algorithms. You need to consistently provide value to both potential customers and Google in everything you do. It mustn't be dismissed, but look to the ever-changing current situation, largely dictated by Google and, if you want to do well online, you need to consistently be doing a better job than your competitors by providing searchers with a better user experience and more relevant, interesting, shareable content.

Always own your own platform - don't rent - as you should not be running your business online through social media or other rented platforms. By investing time in your website and its content, optimising it consistently for performance and augmenting this by investing in areas such as Google My Business, content marketing and social media to drive traffic to your site, you are not only improving your SEO, but you are also taking care of and constantly upgrading your own property. Search engine optimisation is often an investment of time and effort, whereas AdWords is a pure investment of cash, so spend time on your neo-SEO in order to get your business to where you want to be, faster, and potentially at less cost.

Content marketing

"If you do not produce consistently engaging content, then you will not attract the attention and maintain the focus of your target audience. It's an exciting time for content producers, as we have a certain freedom to be creative in pursuing material that cuts through the clutter and really makes an impact," Martijn Roelofs, owner and creative director, Boardinghouse Productions.

Content marketing is the art of pulling in business through attraction, rather than forcing your brand upon potential customers. You are showing the how good your business is, rather than telling them, then holding your audience's attention long enough to build a relationship.

Content marketing is as vast a topic as it sounds, because it covers providing all types of information to potential customers that doesn't necessarily in the first instance look like selling - so it actually gets through to them. If you imagine a sales funnel, collecting many potential customers at the top of the funnel, then completing the sale to the smaller percentage at the other end of the process, with content marketing the funnel is deeper and has more steps than ever before.

You want people to draw potential customers to visit your site who have no intention of buying anything from you today, tomorrow, or even in the next year, then you want to provide them with useful content to ensure they come back again and again, building familiarity with and confidence in your brand. Ideally you want to build a long-term relationship with your business, where they respect you for giving them valuable content and not asking for much of anything in return at that time, other than perhaps the opportunity to communicate further. If you consider what I call the ABCDEF purchasing process, content marketing is still at point A or B: Awareness; Becoming interested, rather than the latter stages: Consideration; (Definite) intent; Evaluation; Finalisation. However, it is a crucial part of promoting businesses and organisations unwilling to invest in it will be left behind the competition.

In most successful instances, through content marketing the prospect will feel they have received value or learned something from consuming the content and it will provide them with more confidence in the source of the content, through the fact a relationship has been built. This experience can help the potential customer look favourably upon the source when a purchase decision is finally made. For example, if you hear a real estate agent on the radio every week speaking sense with authority about the market, then some smart people will look the person up or click on the contact link provided on the radio station's website, or accompanying blog on its social media page when the time eventually comes around to buy a house.

The 'evolved iteration of advertising', content marketing is the creation of things your target audience is interested in, which should usually be published on your business' owned-media and remain relevant, valuable, consistent and on-brand. It also isn't a tactic that you can just turn on and off and hope will be successful. It has to be a mindset that is embraced and encouraged. While not a direct sell, content marketing should still be planned and executed with the endgame of achieving organisational goals. Through the content, over time the best attributes and USPs of the brand should be conveyed in an entirely *subtle* way.

There's no end to the types of content you can create, but the key is to create content that appeals to your target audience, whether it be: blog posts, videos, infographics, images, market research, memes, webinars, documentaries, GIFs, case studies, animations, pictures, interviews or email newsletters. It is for those with patience to play a longer game, willing to target potential customers looking to bond with a brand before a purchase decision is made, which can sometimes be a challenge for marketers when chasing budget to create creative content that could take some time for financial return on investment.

Often a successful way to get started with content marketing is to identify and break down your business activities into separate elements, then determine how each can be portrayed in an interesting way to the audience. For example, a veterinarian practice might include departments for several types of animal, with each having a plethora of stories and issues to cover. Vets can speak about seasonal issues, such as dog heat stroke or chocolate poisoning at Christmas; they can communicate with authority on all its services, from animal relocation to obesity management or parasite control and comment upon trends and issues within the market. And don't forget the main tools a vet has that barely any other type of business can offer: an endless supply of cute and cuddly animals, which prove a huge hit among the population and, more importantly, a vet's target audience - animal lovers.

Blogging
The majority of people use their social media platforms as a means of sharing personal thoughts, rather than owning their own online blog property. Blogging on social media has become particularly popular with the upsurge in video use, plus people becoming more comfortable in front of camera. This is being facilitated even more across platforms such as Instagram Stories, Facebook Live feeds and Snapchat, where more and more people are investing time every day in running their own form of blog. However, even taking into account the easy access to social media 'blogging', the micro-blogging website Tumblr boasts over 426 million active blogs in 2018 and the commitment to blogging outside of social channels continues at an impressive rate.

Blogs should be unique to each business. They have constantly evolved over the years and can take many forms - in fact their very charm can often be how they are differentiated from the next blog. If the statistics behind starting a blog for your business are convincing in terms of traffic, sales and lead generation and if you have made the decision to start a blog for your business, you should always host it on your own website. Those who consume and enjoy it can then sign up for updates where you can collect your audience's data and attract people back to your site through emails or push notifications with every blog upload.

Blogs are a time commitment and often rely upon the knowledge of more time-short senior people in an organisation who usually have the real insight. However, there are many useful benefits to taking the plunge and starting a real blog hosted on your website. One is the fact it is not on a social network, where you effectively borrow land for your content and it usually restricts the amount of your content your audience can see through its desire to sell more ads. Blogs are also another touchpoint on the consumer's purchase decision journey, where they are again seeing your brand and are visiting your content over that of your competitors. The increased traffic and dwell time on your site should also make a real difference to how you rank on Google. Last but not least, adverts are always increasing in cost, so this is an opportunity to increase your organic traffic and potentially reduce your advertising bills. The good news is, with such a large number of companies now with websites created by platforms like WordPress and Wix, the technology is already there and it is easy to get started with simple guides to follow online.

Once you've written your blog and you are happy with it, there is usually benefit from getting someone you trust to proofread it. Then it's time to push your blog out and generate some traction. Always keep in mind the rule of promoting to your specific audience. For example, you can perhaps generate a huge amount of cheap traffic and useless engagement promoting your London-based jewellery blog in Cairo on Facebook, but what is the benefit other than gaining more irrelevant followers? Whereas if you had used that budget to promote to a small audience in Knightsbridge, you might have experienced a fraction of the traffic return, but a few followers who will later become real customers.

Putting some social advertising behind your blog is an instant start for generating engagement. Choose your platforms and audience based upon your target market, as you need to keep an eye on the final goal again: *conversions*. For example, Instagram might be a much better platform for selling clothes than Facebook given the demographic of its users, while Facebook may be cheaper per engagement, but with very poor conversions. However, if it's something that targets a certain business type or job profile, LinkedIn tends to have better results, but the cost-per-click can be many times more than other platforms. If unsure, experiment with a few hundred dollars on one, then the other - have some fun comparing results and getting to know both the social media analytics and your site's Google Analytics. You'll soon get a feel for what is working and what isn't. We have had limited conversion success with highly-concentrated social media boosting within a short timeframe, so I recommend you spread any boosts out over at least a couple of weeks.

At the end of your blog, ask for a re-share and there are other engagement tricks, such as linking to websites or other blogs mentioned within the blogs - then on social media, always ensure you tag those brands.

When we create content, such as blogs for clients, we send them the links to push out through their staff's own social media channels. If you are dealing with the boss or an influential person in the organisation, you can ask them to request all the employees share, which can mean content being disseminated by many employees to a large combined audience.

If you want to go the extra mile, you can use analysis tools like BuzzSumo to keep track of those who share your blog and then you can do a bit of research, find their contact details, thank them and see if they'd like to be sent any of your other content.

This leads us to probably the key element of blogs, which is building a following and the most important element of this is generating subscribers. There are tools such as subscribers.com that will alert people in their browser every time a new blog post is published through a push notification. This happens when people visit your blog and are asked if they want to receive blog notifications - if they say yes, they are subscribed. The notifications work exactly the same way with your web browser as with social media platforms, providing alerts on your screen when someone sends you a message on a social channel.

While it might be considered archaic by some, email marketing is not to be dismissed in all circumstances and blogging is one of the situations where it can work well. People have opted-in to your blog specifically because they value the content. Therefore, they are much more likely to be content when notified by email and on many occasions will save the email until they are in the mood or have the time to give it proper attention. You can collect emails on your blog in a number of ways, such as having the contact form in an easy to spot place on the blog itself, or having a data collection pop up such as Optinmonster, which you can set to appear only when your site visitors are exiting without signing up, to reduce the annoyance factor.

Your on-page data collection form and any other third-party applications you use to gather email leads can be automatically integrated with mailing applications, such as Mailchimp or ActiveCampaign, so the addresses are stored there ready to click and send email updates using their ready-made and adaptable templates. Sending people blogs they have agreed to receive future information on is a long way from the annoying spam emails that bombard our inboxes. When you send the new blogs posts to all your subscribers by email, they can easily opt out in the future by clicking 'unsubscribe'.

Add video to your arsenal
You simply cannot afford to ignore video as a key component of your rich content strategy. The statistics are overwhelmingly convincing across the board, that dollar for dollar, video clips beat all other forms of content. Research agrees videos help people make buying decisions and conversion rates increase considerably when there is video on landing pages. It doesn't need to be a Hollywood blockbuster, but having almost any sort of video that fits your budget is more appealing than having no video - even if it's a series of clips shot from a smartphone. As you know, I am trying to stay away from stats in this book, as many varying and regularly-updated examples can easily

be found in a Google News search, but it is very inviting to do so in this section, given the impressive figures out there proving the power of video in your content marketing strategy. Let's just say you are much more likely to sell your products or services when using videos to promote them.

There are a few relatively recent trends to mention regarding video, with one of them being vertically-shot video, which used to be frowned upon, but is now increasing in popularity, given the high tendency for videos to be viewed on smartphones and on social networks. In addition, videos are much more effective when subtitled, so people can watch them without the sound on. I'm sure this format has bloomed in popularity thanks to people who are meant to be working and don't want to give the game away to their boss or are viewing videos in other situations where polite society might raise an eyebrow.

Coming back to budget, you can pay a freelancer or agency to create videos for you. You can negotiate a monthly package and remain flexible around their other commitments. It can also help maximise the use of their time, by being extra-prepared and shooting a number of clips all in one go. Short clips work well and producers, quite rightly, charge based upon time, so by being organised and creative you can put together a bank of professionally-shot clips in one session in order to maximise your budget. If the budget isn't there, then why not try building your, or a colleague's, personal brand with self-shot clips that maintain personality and authenticity. Become a known face and voice as a thought leader in your field - what have you go to lose? You can create videos such as Q&As, recorded webinars, live interviews, product reviews and demonstrations, plus you can live stream from presentations at events or conferences, to name but a few scenarios.

One of the most frustrating challenges faced in our industry is encouraging clients to invest more in video for events. Often a video can cost as little as five per cent of the activity it would showcase, but one could argue it can double the value when done well. There is a plethora of photographers and videographers of all levels and prices offering professional options that can be worked into a budget, from basic and raw to television-standard with animation. The uses for this type of content are many and powerful, so there's no excuse for undervaluing this important element of your communications mix. I always say: once the event money is spent, the laughter has died and the team is cleaning up, you have little left to show for it and to use in the future if you haven't invested in a video clip.

Native advertising
Born from the fact consumers increasingly reject adverts and publishers have to find more intricate, clever ways to be profitable, native advertising is an increasingly important avenue for businesses to promote themselves. Consumers of native adverts, whether in the written, visual or audio form, are generally open to being advertised to in this way, as long as they are clearly labelled as such.

Generally native advertising is a form of paid advertising, but the advertising is complementary to the media format in which it appears. Unlike display advertising, the best native adverts often don't really look like adverts at all and, as such, are generally much more successful. The most common in-feed native adverts are the type you can't avoid seeing on your social feeds, which make them among the easiest to initiate, but also crude, not incredibly creative and often quite expensive per-click.

Then there are 'recommended content' adverts, where you might watch a clip and then you are recommended to watch something else. Platforms facilitating this type of native advertising, such as AdSense, Outbrain and Taboola, have gathered popularity as simpler routes to distribute content, bringing potential customers to content they didn't know they were looking for. For example, if a consumer is watching a global news clip about electronic surfboards, they might then be attracted to click on a video advert for your brand electronic surfboard featuring one of the world's top surfers when it automatically appears alongside it.

If there are online publications you know are perfect for your target audience, you can always contact them directly to devise and negotiate a form of native advertising that will work for your brand. This can be time consuming and is another area in which having an agency working on your behalf can help broker the best deal and deliver the right messaging.

Most large global brands now run native campaigns of some sort. The best forms of native advertising are when brands really dig deep creatively and create campaigns in which they pull in their target audience in interesting and fun ways. 2018's Webby Award winner for best use of native advertising was M&M's & Friends. The chocolate brand's campaign aimed to move away from 50 years of television advertising and reach its audience in a new way. Highly creative native advertising was a novel way to use the brand's ultra-colourful sugar-coated cartoon characters in a user-generated Instagram comic strip. The Instagram followers of M&M's were asked to post pictures with the campaign hashtag and some photographs would be selected by some clever artists to turn into an ongoing comic. Followers began to take and post pictures specifically in an attempt to have their photograph become the next edition of the comic. Largely through entrants tagging other friends, M&M's quickly added over 120,000 engaged followers to its Instagram page, all through an initiative that cost very little to execute.

Experiment and analyse results using different forms of native advertising, as get it right and it can deliver impressive traffic and brand awareness for minimal cost-per-click. However, ensure you are completely happy with your content, as it will not perform well if it is not relevant, engaging and doesn't give your audience the desire to share. Try and keep the content as niche as possible, directed at your target audience and always keeping your final objectives in mind.

Podcasts
This is an area that has experienced rapid recent growth and is predicted for continued upsurge over coming years. To put it into perspective, it was reported almost $330 million would be spent in the US on podcast advertising in 2018. The beauty of podcasts is how they are so niche and can exactly hit a brand's target market. Take for example a podcast on children's health - this could be a fantastic platform for an international chain of nursery schools,

whether they are hosting it, or sponsoring another's show. Therefore, if you have the type of business and talent to pull off a podcast, then it is definitely an avenue to keep in mind, as more and more people add specialist podcasts to their subscriber lists for their gym workouts, travelling or while simply driving their daily commute.

Apart from the obvious marketing benefits to getting involved with specialist podcasts, there can also be impressive website traffic page ranking benefits, as you can often have the might of iTunes and Google Play linking to your website because you are mentioned on a popular podcast's blurb.

If you decide to commit the time resource to begin your own podcast, rather than pay to get involved with an existing one, then it has similar benefits to running your own blog from your website: you then own the online real estate and all the benefits this brings. If it is a success the rewards can be huge in terms of awareness, web traffic and the potential of you even generating your own advertising income from the podcast.

The podcast can be promoted in the same ways as a blog. Running a regular podcast, especially with exciting and well-respected guests who can share among their own audiences, can be a powerful form of content, especially if you transcribe the content and then use this for further content marketing.

Remarketing content
Despite its drawback in terms of lower conversion rates, many sources believe display advertising is growing at a faster rate than PPC, and remarketing is playing a big part

in this. This practice of what is essentially 'cyberstalking' potential customers with ads after they've browsed a site is often adopted simply because it works. And its effectiveness shouldn't be surprising, given it is such an impressive tool to exploit one of the oldest fundamentals of advertising - around seven touchpoints to generate a viable lead - as remarketing is an accelerated way of achieving these touchpoints.

The deviously technical nature of remarketing might put you off trying this yourself, but don't be deterred, as with any globally-effective form of advertising, there is a plethora of software companies out there providing simple user interfaces, taking the pain out of setting up and managing your remarketing requirements. As always, it is a good place to start looking at Google and its AdWords remarketing solution, which has tutorials and step-by-step instructions to add the required tag to your website, then you are up and running on the Google Display Network. Social networks such as Facebook and LinkedIn provide their own remarketing solutions and there are applications such as AdRoll, which works with a variety of networks and handles the technical aspects of your remarketing - for a fee of course. There are also link retargeting solutions from providers such as RetargetLinks and Rebrandly where you create a short link with them and then when it is shared through content marketing methods, whether it be social media, a blog, email campaign or podcast, those who click the link will begin to see your banner ads.

Your own business and target audience must always drive your content marketing choices. In addition, most things to be done properly will have a cost involved, even if it is a time cost and not financial. However, don't take the decision to making a time commitment lightly, as most content marketing requires consistency in the amount of content produced and the timings of release. Humans are creatures of habit and if you get it right and your audience enjoys your podcast, blog, quiz or video clips, then you can build much more momentum by doing them regularly, rather than sporadically.

To put the value of content marketing into perspective, there are millions of blogs reportedly published daily. Blogging has become a necessity for so many types of business to generate sales as an alternative to paying for ads. As we consume increasing amounts of content through our smartphones and specifically through social feeds, it will continue to become increasingly important, as brands need potential customers to have eyeballs on *their* content over their competitors. Always ensure your content is targeted to your audience, reflects your brand values and remains consistent.

Event marketing

"Event marketing is a crucial aspect of most events. From the moment the event or exhibition is confirmed, the communication between the organisers and the marketing team is key to maximising its success and ensuring amplification of its messages," **Robyn Sokol, MD, Emerald Events & Exhibitions.**

We have reached the final discipline, but don't relax as you're not off the hook yet. I am not going to lighten things up with a section on how to throw a good party. However, we wouldn't have covered all the main communications avenues for promoting your business without giving advice for those times when remote forms of marketing may not be enough, or you simply feel it is time to physically engage your target audience at the human level. In our world of social media interaction, teleconferences, WhatsApp groups and ever-lengthening multi-party email chains, we have seen clients generate huge benefits in terms of true networking, goodwill-building and powerful widespread exposure earned through strategic, integrated events and activations marketing.

Our agency handles events for both business-to-business and business-to-consumer clients, from industries as varied as telecommunications, to facilities management, online currencies, insurance, legal, art and architecture. We even deliver regular 'out of this world' networking events for the world's leading satellite operator. While there are many types of event, from presentations to thought-leadership sessions, webinars and workshops, there are three types of activation that perform particularly well for business-to-business marketing: platform opportunities, corporate networking events and roundtables. It is particularly true in organisations that are targeting other businesses, that people like to buy from people and there's no better way to facilitate this. The events and the fresh content that comes with them also act as a newsworthy catalyst for PR, which of course keeps our PR team satisfied, because they have strong stories to pitch to the media and the creative team also gets major traction with dynamic content they can produce and disseminate on social media.

As an example, because we have many clients in the construction, engineering and technical services industry, we organised a roundtable on the topic of sustainability, which included a number of leaders from their respective fields and the Principal from the university in which we held the event. Largely comprised of our clients and prospective clients, all seven guest speakers could potentially do business with each other and the topic was of interest to the main trade publications, national newspapers and even newswires, such as Reuters. We knew the target media were interested in the event, because we involved them from the outset, asking them for their endorsement and suggestions before deciding upon the final topics.

We organised the attendees, which included pitching the concept, ensuring their confirmation, then some coaching on how they could contribute. On the day, we decided to differentiate the event from other roundtables through making it a 'standing' event, due to the school of thought that it focuses and energises discussion by standing up, rather than sitting comfortably on a seat, or behind a desk. A simple USP like this and well-thought-out pitch ensured all our preferred attendees made the early morning event, which began at 8am to cause minimum disruption to the calendars of the busy executives. Several key media attended, and we prepared a skeleton press release in advance of the event with a strong writer assigned the task of finalising it later with the main newsline or 'golden nugget' from the event and some 'colour' from the discussions had. We had branding in place for pictures, some refreshments and allowed time for mingling between the speakers before and after the event. We engaged the marketing teams of all the organisations well in advance and they knew to expect content coming through social channels, as we had a photographer, video producer and social media manager all in position and briefed to ensure the highlights were captured and pushed out during the event.

The press release went out on the day and some of the PR team were primed to call the key journalists who were already alerted to expect it to come through as early as possible. It is key to get news articles out in the first half of the day, as the daily news media tend to decide what will go in and what won't during their daily news conferences -

normally one late morning, then another in the afternoon. Consider it this way - if news titles go to print that evening and you provide a strong story late in the day, then it is disruptive and they only have a few hours to work on it, so they are more likely to opt for another story they have had more time to do justice.

We had an excellent MC who knew the industry and some of speakers running the schedule, making the formal introductions, maintaining the topic flow and controlling the questions from the audience. Best-laid plans to keep it within around an hour quickly went out the window, as the speakers clearly appreciated the opportunity to discuss and indeed vent their opinions on key industry topics, creating truly powerful and somewhat controversial news. In addition to the goodwill, impressive networking opportunity and engaging visual content generated during the event, the PR value also went through the roof as stories from the discussion hit the headlines, including over 50 pieces of news coverage amounting to over half a million online coverage views, including a front-page leading story in one of the main national newspapers. The story must also have landed on the desk, laptop or smartphone of someone influential, as one of the pieces of national legislation criticised by the experts during the event as hindering environmental sustainability was withdrawn within 48 hours of the story being published. In addition, there were several thousand organic social media post engagements on the day from within the country, all attributed to the event. Of course, there was a hashtag assigned for everything related to the event, which was chosen way back in the planning stage and included in all creative and content. This 'standing' roundtable event was a cost-effective example of the use of simple event marketing and integrated communications to deliver brand awareness, thought leadership, personal branding and targeted networking.

As with every element of marketing, spend time on your strategy, considering: what is the ideal result and how should you frame the entire experience and mould the process to get there? After you have identified the correct attendees, you should begin generating excitement for your event well in advance through a pre-event content plan where you can also create more interest among the target audience. Your audience is key, so spend some time identifying the best online channels and tactics to reach them. You need to know exactly what you want to get out of your event in order to build a solid strategy to get the right people involved and the correct messaging to the target audience.

While there should be an endgame in mind, being pushy with sales at an event is off-putting, as people generally don't convert on the first interaction, so it's important to generate awareness and excitement in the lead up to your event. Give yourself enough time to promote the value of your event and your potential attendees enough time to plan and register.

Research the material for the event well and ensure everything is tailored with the attendees in mind. Consider the industries, companies, roles, and seniority of those attending and ensure your content is relevant to them. You want people to walk away with actionable advice and to feel like you have brought value to their professional lives, or there could be an aftertaste of resentment, through perceived time wastage. If they can't trust you to deliver exactly what they were expecting at the initial event, then how can the relationship move forward into a formal relationship - first impressions last.

Events are usually a costly option to pursue, certainly in terms of time resource, so ensure there is a value-add follow-up at a later date, which can be a subtle way to keep the conversation going. Post-event communications are key to keeping the conversation going and maximising the impact of your investment. You need to be strategic in how you work with your sales team to maximise event return on investment. Perhaps it is the later delivery of a video summary of the event, pictures, media coverage, or a guide to implementing a topic discussed. The conversation has taken place and the interest is hopefully already piqued, so this is a great way to add extra value post-event and maintain the relationship.

Here are some points to consider for your next event marketing opportunity:

Go 'live'
By their very category, events are living, moving, lively organisms, so plan whatever ways you can to bring in dynamic, responsive marketing elements. Your event marketing may have worked and you have a full house, but the numbers in the building should only be a fraction of the size of audience that should know and learn about the event, its content and even - if video is produced - see it. It is crucial you continue to continue promoting the event throughout its duration to maintain and maximise its potential reach.

Consider live streaming your event, or at least the keynotes or highlights of it. Set up a live feed from the event, or at least some of the juicy parts, which is simple to do through platforms, such as Facebook and YouTube. There are even other third-party applications in the unlikely event you don't have social channels to utilise. Then once it is finished, you can post the video and even send it to attendees. However, sourcing a professional microphone and video camera setup is advised, which shouldn't be cost-restrictive, as they can be rented. Also, obtain a non-public WIFI feed from the venue, as we have found a packed room can reduce strength to the degree that the live feed can suffer. This is recorded-live feed is another great chance to collect legacy material to use when promoting the next big event.

Ensure the event hashtag is ubiquitous throughout the event and have the MC mentions it every single time they start a new section. It's much better if the hashtag and the content becomes part of the conversation itself, such as a means of asking questions for a panel, giving feedback to the discussions, or even if it is a way of winning prizes in engagement competitions. Task your own team with generating some interesting content using the hashtag for the attendees to easily retweet and share on their channels. You should be engaging with all of the audience's input - there is no excuse for a wasted opportunity. It can be obvious whether the person tasked with this during-event hashtag engagement is enjoying it or not, by the quantity and quality of content, plus the general tone and creativity in the messaging, responses and conversations. In addition, always be ready with some approved advertising budget to gather some wider external momentum throughout the event.

Partner power

Okay, so you are delivering some engaging content about the event on your company's social channels, but is everyone involved? What about the 20 speakers and panellists, other partners, venue, sponsors and attendees? How are they being encouraged to spread the messages as widely as possible? Everyone's involved for a somehow-related reason, so it's likely there is an impressive shared target audience among everyone involved. If you haven't even attempted to reach this audience through the event stakeholders, then you have failed in your event marketing this time around.

The potential reach of your event partners is always an element to consider in the event planning stage. Provided their own social audience is aligned with your target audience, why not build their posting activities into your strategy and the contract or deliverables you agree with them?

If they are of the right profile, it is always a good idea to secure one-on-one interviews with the event partners across all types of media, with the popular radio stations and local TV news channels in particular always open to a pitch for a visiting speaker, celebrity or expert in their field. Remember, if you want the monthly trade publications or even newspapers to run a substantial piece on them that promotes the event, then you need to organise PR activity well in advance.

Be experiential

Whether you are harnessing the latest artificial intelligence technology, creating interactive workshops, employing ice-breaking or team building activities, or hiring entertainment or a gimmick for your event, making it as experiential as possible can provide attendees with unforgettable memories and associate your brand with that element for many years to come.

In today's global economy, being truly unique is often one of the toughest things to achieve. It can be even more tricky with corporate events, as many attendees will be in a position within their organisation where they attend many similar types of events. However, just because it's difficult doesn't mean it needs to be expensive, or that you should ignore trying to make your event stand out from the rest. For example, the iHC 'standing' roundtable is perhaps remembered by its participants for the fact that, despite having to stand up for the whole event, they didn't want the debate to end, carrying it on long after the time was up. The experience was a first for them and helped us gain more interest from our event marketing activities.

Another example is when we organised a large high-level global financial event where we brought in handheld voting technology, so the audience could give their opinion on predetermined topics discussed by the industry leaders on the stage. These vote results were then pushed out live above the stage on a big screen, through social media, to traditional media using a press release and by the global newswire media correspondent in attendance.

Michael Jackson posthumously 'performed' at the 2014 Billboard Music Awards, in holographic form, which grabbed all the headlines, both good and bad, but created global news and incredible social media numbers for the event, which wouldn't otherwise have happened. Even for those who attended, if you ask them now to tell you the first thing they remember about it, it's unlikely to be the winner of Top Rap Artist.

Also consider all of the event partners and if they have any potentially exciting experiential collaterals they can bring to the event and display as a point of interest. They will probably jump at the chance to gain extra and free exposure for their brand. If you have a representative from Porsche speaking at your automotive event and the car producer has just released an incredible new multi-million-dollar concept supercar, then ask them if they would like to bring it along – it would certainly cause a buzz in the foyer.

Foster fun
Whether it is a hackathon or brainstorming session to get the creative juices flowing; a team building exercise for bonding, a quiz, ice-breaker game or an entertainment performance that appeals to the target audience, try and always add a fun element to your event. From our event marketing experience, real bonds and lasting relationships are formed, plus more organic social sharing and word-spreading, when the networking is enjoyable for those involved.

'Did someone say after-party, or was it pre-party?' We have seen a real move towards our clients pulling budget out of costly exhibition stands and putting it into more tactical, networking social events. Many events, conferences, exhibitions and seminars can be dry and not entirely dissimilar from the same one that happened the year before, or a month earlier in another country. Therefore, providing an off-site party to unwind after the event is more often becoming a serious consideration as a strategic alternative.

For example, we held an after-party for a leading international architecture client after the final day of a global real estate exhibition. As part of the glitzy bash, we hired a professional comedian as MC, brought onboard a well-known DJ, laid on high-quality food and drinks and designed the entire nearby venue in the branding style of the client. This was all done for a fraction of the cost of the client exhibiting, so instead they attended the exhibition during the day and were able to invite along key clients and targets to their after-party. This provided a priceless non-formal, face-to-face marketing opportunity for the company, even attracting international VIP attendees and 'sealing some deals' in the process. Another often-overlooked concept is the event pre-party, where those attending an event can get together for some networking prior to the event. Creating some buzz in advance can also be a good way of getting some last-minute registrations in for the event itself.

To ensure the success of your event marketing, you can employ the integrated communications principles we have previously covered:

Planning
As soon as the event is confirmed, get everyone involved together to brainstorm and lay out every single detail of the event, breaking it up into all the individual elements, from theme, to venue, speakers and topics, and then decide upon your communications objectives from the event. Within your strategy, create subsections for all the elements we have mentioned in this book. Then decide

upon those elements that you will employ and who is responsible for each task. A detailed scope of work can then be created so everyone knows what will happen and when. This scope also should include advertising budgets, channels and timings, as required.

Once the event plan is drafted, it is important to get everyone together again to go through the integrated communications strategy and give their input, as there is no way you will have captured everything at the first attempt. At this stage, the power of the 'collective' will ensure a much more detailed and creative strategy is set early in the process, giving a higher chance of success and better goal-setting. Then, again assign and resource all the deliverables required in order to achieve the plan and ensure the events objectives are surpassed.

Integrated communications
Events are usually the best opportunities to use all the marketing channels available at your fingertips in choreographed unison. All of these tactics directed together can create powerful results, but this requires heavily investing in the work up-front to produce the detailed strategy.

Your event hashtag is the common factor that pulls together all your communications and, with the strategy agreed and everyone assigned their roles, the only way this will now fall down is through poor communication and lack of teamwork. Have the event team meet regularly in the run up to the event and ensure a WhatsApp group, Google Drive or Cloud folder and other preferred communications platforms are live, so everyone involved has a common storage facility and platform for discussion.

Traditional PR
Events is an area where PR can work particularly well, as implicitly they have some newsworthy value as something physical is actually happening and effort has been put in to create something both 'new' and engaging. A simple way to maximise and extend your all-important event PR is to break down the interesting elements of the event, consider stories or pitch points around these interesting elements and then segregate your planning into pre, during and post activity.

Pre-event PR:
Regardless of whether it is a public or private event, the very process of putting together a draft event 'anchor press release' helps lay the foundation for the event's public relations. Agreeing all of the finer details, including the 5Ws & How of an event, helps firm up the communications process and gives the team the parameters for creativity around the key messages. This anchor release should have a headline and newsline based upon the main selling or unique point of the event, such as 'January Electronics Event Set to Break World Record for Shopping Bargains', then the release should provide all the information that explains the headline. At the end of the release, most events will also include who can attend, the price and where to buy the tickets or reserve the place, including links when possible.

I personally find it simpler to get all the information we have down into the press release first, then decide the headline from what appears to be the most interesting element, or newsline, of the story, then rearranging the information accordingly. It is also often a good exercise to perform early, as the process can sometimes identify gaps in information that can be relayed back to the event planners. A good way to get started on this process is to research Google News and find the way your bullseye target publication has previously reported similar types of event. This identifies the best examples of the how your target media likes to receive the information and will also give you a guide to structuring the release and highlight elements you may not otherwise have thought of including.

Create a list of media and influencers you would like to receive invitations and receive the press release. Then separate a hitlist from this larger list, identifying the most important contacts to whom you should verbally pitch the pre-event release and invite to attend. It is possible you will not have these contacts, which is one of the reasons why PR companies are so widely used for event marketing and play an important role in making them a success. However, with some serious effort invested in online research, telephone and email work, you can begin to fulfil this role - but don't underestimate the time commitment it takes to do it right, and don't bank on a journalist who confirms attendance two months prior to an event to remember to show up. Reminders and re-confirmations nearer event time are compulsory, regardless of how keen someone sounded when you first pitched the event to them. Start the media outreach early and have a few conversations with key contacts in order to build genuine interest in the event over time. We asked a number of journalists how they preferred to receive their pitches and it was a resounding: email, then phone at a later date, always personalised messages and the newsline has to be targeted at their own audience. Don't forget relevant listings and event calendars, which can drive search engine traffic to your event - simply search for similar events in the area to find them.

During-event PR:
Have someone assigned to look after the media and influencers you have attending, coordinating interviews and chasing up those who haven't arrived. Often those who confirm later discover they can't make it when other stories break at the same time. However, if you are proactive and develop a relationship, they will usually happily run something based upon the information you subsequently provide them.

From the material of those presenting and the event's planned content, we usually have the skeleton of a release ready to send on the day before the event even happens. Generally, this 'draft release' will be added to on the morning of the event and sent out to media and influencers from the event, along with a professionally-taken news picture. These on-the-day releases do particularly well when some of the key media are expecting it on the day - and they should be if you have done a thorough job of the pre-event invitations and pitching.

For media in attendance, prepare a list of potential interviewees from the speakers and organisers and have pitch points prepared for media in attendance. Depending on the event, you should have a press pack prepared with press releases, bios, pictures and clips, which can be given to the media and influencers in attendance and potentially increase the amount of coverage generated.

Post-event PR:
Keep track of media who you expect to publish from your event. Media professionals and influencers are busy people and some stories will often drop down their priority list. By offering to help them along the way and reminding them you are available to help, it can keep your story top of mind with them in the weeks following the event - just try and not irritate them, or they might blacklist you.

There are often plenty of potential post-event stories. For instance, we will release information about any major contract signings after a business development event, which can generate widespread coverage for the company and the event, depending upon the project size. It is also best practice to reach out to speakers and selected attendees and ask if they had any successful outcomes from the event, which will build real credibility for future events and produce an online legacy of success.

PR+
Have the process well-planned for social media dissemination, ensuring everyone knows - from the immediate team, to the partners, speakers and attendees - which content should be expected and when in order to encourage sharing. Establish a formal system for sharing and amplifying media coverage, with these responsibilities clearly allocated. Break through the inevitable uncertainty and possessiveness that happens when working across brands and instil confidence that you consider everyone's success as the priority – not just that of the event.

Social media marketing

Use engaging visuals, videos and animations to draw attention to your posts from the event. Many of these can be pre-planned or prepared prior to the event. Establish a budget for social media advertising, to extend the reach and awareness of the event and ensure as many of your target audience is engaged as possible.

Influencer marketing
Whether or not the media interest in the event is strong, you should also identify a hit list of influencers to approach with a proposition for the event. The type of influencer you can approach may depend upon the budget, but if the topic is suited to their channel and audience, then it may be easier than you think to get them excited, especially if you can get them involved in the format somehow. Remember, most influencers are usually keen to listen to opportunities to promote their own brand, and your event might just offer them this.

Online advertising
In particular there might be onsite opportunities or media partnerships that can be sealed for your event, bringing impressive paid-for exposure and, if you get the pitch right, even some bartered PR exposure. This can be an option to consider with a media channel that wasn't interested in the event from an editorial perspective, but is particularly important in terms of reaching the target audience and event objectives.

Neo-SEO
You should consider a website or microsite - particularly for events that will repeat. Once optimised for data capture, you can use various neo-SEO techniques to drive traffic and then strategically remarket to your audience.

Your own online property is where you should be driving all your hard-earned event traffic, so it is important all the details are there, from timings, to agenda, speakers and travel details, including clickable links for attendees to book tickets, reserve their spot or ask for more information.

The use of third-party listings can also be a great source of web traffic for event marketing, where you can drive traffic back to your site, then capture their details, using data capture software and storing this vital information for future communications. Again, searches on Google of similar events should return the most relevant listings for your event.

Content marketing
If you don't record powerful imagery and create reusable content during the event then you can't use it to promote the next event, so plan ahead and invest in quality video and photography you can reuse many times over. If hiring an experienced professional or agency is outside your budget, then perhaps get in touch with a local university and ask if any multimedia students want the experience - you'll find most have equipment and will appreciate the opportunity to build their portfolio.

Throughout the pre, during and post-event process, a blog or news section can keep people returning and momentum building. It is key to leverage the content and interest that can be gleaned from the speakers or exhibitors. On most occasions the entire content marketing plan can be built around the star attractions of an event. Take for example 'Big Boys Toys', a large annual exhibition of the latest gadgets targeting men with high disposable income, ranging from the latest supercars and marine craft, to advanced consumer electronics. Tasked with building an integrated communications plan, we generated millions of dollars of global media coverage for the event, including a packed press conference, through focusing almost entirely on the exhibitors and their products. Each already had their own fantastic content, from videos of supercars or giant robots in action, to pictures of futuristic watch designs, and it was our job to collect it and strategically plan its use for the event's marketing.

Email marketing
It doesn't get much more niche than an event, which is the reason email marketing works so well and, as such, is a must for event marketing. You must develop a separate email marketing plan in advance of sending emails, as by approaching email marketing strategically, you will not only have more success, but will also demonstrate that the event is well organised to the recipients. It will also make this crucial part of your event less of a headache and much easier to resource, to the extent you can schedule some pre-planned emails, using user-friendly software, such as MailChimp and ActiveCampaign, to send automatically along the way, so long as your databases remain up to date, as differently targeted emails will be required for different lists.

Consider an email blast at the top of your funnel, where you have a database that would be interested in your event. This will spread awareness and, hopefully, produce some enquiries about the event. We usually maintain a 'target' list of those we want to attract to the event and 'confirmed' list of those who have already committed to going, as the communications should be tailored differently. A useful tip is to email a calendar event to all those who have confirmed, so they can easily save it on their smartphone and set a reminder 48 hours before.

After the event, it can be a nice touch to email your attendees with pictures and other images or footage from the event. People can't resist looking for themselves in event pictures, particularly if you have included a branded photo opportunity wall or booth at the event, where many attendees love to pose, capture, and share the moment. And, don't forget to add your own messaging into this final event communication.

Epilogue

Promoting Your Business will be updated and completely re-written annually, published three weeks prior to the start of each year in order to maximise its relevance and usefulness for both returning and new readers.

As you now know, at a later stage in the several months it took to write this, I decided to add a chapter on planning. It was an afterthought then and now it's appearing again in my summary. Working in the marketing and communications industries for over two decades, I chose a career that neither supports with my aversion to chaos, nor my complete inability to multitask. I have been hands-on involved in all elements of these facets of 'promoting your business', but usually with a strong team of specialists and fantastically motivated, applied and professional people around me. If you are a small business owner reading this, or even an employee beamed into the task of 'sorting out' the marketing of one of the many larger companies, where their marketing and communications fell behind due to rapid growth of the company - do not be daunted.

Sitting reading this might bring a similar feeling to the one an owner of an agency gets when, after months of hard chasing, suddenly lands three big new contracts - with everything needing to start yesterday. Your biggest ally is planning. Use this book as a checklist to ensure you have covered most elements. Perhaps put the headings throughout the book onto a spreadsheet – or start scribbling notes as you work your way through it. Nearly every part should form the beginning of your research into each discipline, not the end. Document when you want everything to happen and then work one day at a time to deliver a powerful integrated communications plan, which will have all around you impressed and the competition asking each other what the hell has happened over at your company - because your brand is now 'everywhere'.

Your competition isn't marketing themselves better because they are smarter than you, or because they are just brilliant at doing things ad-hoc. Some time ago they or the agency they hired merely spent some time laying their integrated strategy out and assigned the right people to deliver each part. It often takes planning, organisation, time and the courage to be bold to deliver disruptive marketing. However, by employing all these tactics, you can make great leaps forward and achieve remarkable results for your business.

Rather like this book, which seemed like a distant dream for me to make the time to write - if you don't begin then you'll never get there. I hope it helps you and perhaps acts as a springboard for you to dive into the book's elements in more detail, promote your business better and achieve your goals, whatever they are.

About the author

At the turn of the millennium, I began my journey into marketing through PR as a fresh-faced business economics graduate from the University of Glasgow and IT postgraduate from the University of Aberdeen. Throughout my academic years I had been marked down for my writing being 'too journalistic'. Therefore, upon graduation and having no clue which career I truly wanted to pursue, the idea came to try my hand at journalism. To get the ball rolling, I joined the team at The University of Aberdeen's student newspaper, The Gaudie, and was soon enjoying writing various types of features, such as a report from an intrepid expedition to find the Loch Ness Monster. While it may have all seemed like a bit of fun, it also got me hooked on writing and having my work read by a large number of people - The Gaudie is well-read by the sizeable university population of over 14,000, which seemed a lot then. Ready for career progression, I used this as a stepping stone to land an internship with the local publisher, Aberdeen Journals, where I received some training in news writing with their daily regional broadsheet, The Press & Journal and evening city tabloid, the Evening Express.

I arrived at the enormous open plan newsroom, largely covering stories that no one else could be bothered with. The first by-line I wrote was one I gleaned from a customer at my evening bar job who was up in arms about kids setting fire to communal bins in the housing scheme where he lived. Cue the picture of a furious chap standing beside fire-blackened industrial-size bins and my by-line name beside the surprisingly large article, for all the city to read in the popular evening newspaper. The traineeship was during a cold dark Aberdeen winter and I somehow managed to quickly develop a reputation as the kid who would stand outside the supermarket in the freezing cold and solicit written vox pops (people's opinions recorded while talking informally in a public place) and headshot pictures from shivering parents as they pushed their trolleys to their car, while trying to control their screaming kids. After several weeks I was delighted to be offered a full-time traineeship and I do remember deliberating over a choice between this job and one at DC Thomson's Dundee Courier newspaper, which also produces national treasures like The Dandy and The Beano.

However, a part of me felt the position might be restrictive in career terms and I might not be making the most of my five years of university education. I also clearly remember an endless supply of press releases hitting the news desk, mostly by fax, and thinking it seems more powerful to get a story into several media than writing an article that generally only appears in one. I convinced myself of the 'power of PR' and felt this was the best career option at the time. It didn't harm the decision that one of the agencies I was speaking to about a position was handling corporate PR for the local professional football team, which, being a big fan of the sport, I thought would be both a fun and valuable experience. I have to say, it still impresses me how those running the local PR agencies used to keep tabs on the new junior reporters on the news desk, to see if they could be a valuable recruit for them. I remember one reporter telling me she had been asked about my abilities by the local head of Weber Shandwick and she had told them: 'He seems very competent'. At least she didn't get too carried away with my potential.

After much deliberation between the newspapers and the interested PR agencies, I decided to jump ship to what many journalists still call 'the dark side' by taking up a position at PR agency Beattie Media's small Aberdeen office – yes, the one that handled Aberdeen Football Club's PR, even though it came with even lower salary than other offers. I worked at Beattie for over a year before moving to the Falkirk office, servicing Glasgow and Edinburgh, dealing with accounts including commercial property and, somewhat bizarrely, a shopping mall in Sunderland. It soon became obvious the daily car commute from my apartment in the west end of Glasgow was too much travelling and I moved back to Aberdeen, where I landed a poorly paid, but incredibly fun position as the PR executive for the tourist board, promoting Aberdeen and Grampian Highlands tourism, which comprises largely castles, whisky, hotels and restaurants, which it claimed to be worth over £500 million annually to the area. As chief press officer for the organisation, responsible for all news-related promotion and corporate PR, the position lent me the freedom to do whatever it took to generate my own news stories – which somehow led me to dressing up three times for the picture opportunity. Dressed in a Gandalf The Grey outfit, complete with beard, pointy hat and stick, I generated some solid publicity for the Spirit of Speyside Walking Festival, with some silhouette pictures taken on a hilltop of some little people walking behind the great wizard with backpacks on – well it is a journey after all. On another story I managed to source the outfit of a giant biting midge, after seeing it at a trade fair promoting a machine that literally sucked the flies out of the air. From some 'creative' online research, the newsline of my story was the east coast midge isn't as aggressive as the west coast midge, contrary to popular understanding. The stunt generated a lot of publicity, including an interview on Terry Wogan's BBC2 radio show, which was the most listened to in the country at that time. However, I am sure it got my boss at the time into hot water for approving it, as the tourist board on the west coast didn't appreciate the comparison and kicked up a bit of a fuss. Another story claiming Aberdeen was in fact the sunniest city in the UK generated national publicity, which was helped by a picture set up of some happy young ladies frolicking in the beach in bikinis – a story that had particular success in the all-powerful UK national tabloids. There were lots of these fun stories, including haggis hunting season, coldest place in Britain and other newslines devised to draw media attention to the area.

However, in 2004 a letter was left on my desk from the hand of the city's Lord Provost about a book that had been written tracing Elvis Presley's lineage to a man from a village called Lonmay. The newshound in me immediately saw the story, but no one could have expected the tornado of publicity that was about to hit the east coast of Scotland. I invited the author, Allan Morrison, up for a photo opportunity and, after failing to find an Elvis impersonator on my meagre budget, I hired a fancy-dress outfit complete with wig and glasses, then invited the local news agency along to the sleepy village. After being released on the newswires, the story quickly gathered momentum - appearing in UK newspapers and on some national broadcast bulletins. Then some international newswires picked it up and before long it was a trending story globally – hitting all the major newspapers, in many languages, from the Washington Post to the Sydney Morning Herald. People at breakfast tables all over the world were opening their newspapers to the picture of myself jumping in the air 'rocking' some bagpipes, badly dressed as The King. My phone barely stopped ringing for days and the only public house in Lonmay was soon fully booked for weeks due largely to international media covering the story. It seemed the world had been waiting a long time for a fresh Elvis angle and news crews flew into the village, while the author did a tour of the national UK breakfast TV shows. It was quite an incredible result for the region and the articles can still easily be found on Google to this day. It was also a lesson that each story should be approached in a thorough way, as while some might not garner much interest, from time to time it can blow up and priceless PR is the result.

These tourist board stories were all my own ideas to draw as much media attention as possible to the region's tourism offering and they did generate incredible amounts of publicity for the area without any real budget. Looking back, it was an ideal job to develop skills delivering creative, proactive public relations. During this 2003-2005 period, I was also involved in PR for the Scottish Film Tourism Liaison Group, plus Ski Scotland and would organise press trips for journalists to come and explore the activities, fine cuisine and, of course, the wares of the world-famous Speyside whisky distilleries.

However, it was time to get serious and, at the tender age of 27, I was offered the position of Deputy Head of

Communications for Grampian Police, where I headed the regional force's busy media office. There I led the team, reacting to constant daily calls from media and proactively promoting the force's many initiatives and campaigns - from road safety to crime reduction. Supervising up to 15 press releases a day, fielding an average of 50 calls and arranging around five photo opportunities per week, this position was a huge leap in terms of work intensity and responsibility and prepared me well for future career challenges. For example, one day a child had went missing and rumours began to spread of potential abduction. When this happens some of the world's media begins to contact the press office, in case they are looking at a child murder story. Press conferences were held and regular media updates went out, while some alarming police records of one of the child's guardians were kept from the public, despite the clamour for information. This turned out to be the correct decision, as the child has merely stayed over at a friend's house and had not told anyone their whereabouts. The role was a steep learning curve in the power of the media, how to work under severe pressure and the potential consequences of providing information. During my time with the police I am proud to have created a community engagement anti-vandalism campaign which we as a team worked hard to deliver, using all elements of integrated communications tactics available at that time and bringing on board all the main daily newspapers, radio and television stations, plus uniting politicians and departments of the local council and other public organisations along the way in the cause. The campaign, which reduced vandalism in the city by 17 per cent and was mentioned in parliament on two separate occasions, won the UK Best Strategic PR

Campaign Award, beating all the major police forces, such as London Metropolitan, despite their extensive resources.

In under two years with the police, I was given the opportunity of a holiday to Dubai in the United Arab Emirates, to consider it as a place to live and work, thanks to family living there. Therefore, I decided to jet out for a holiday and test the job market, lining up some interviews and having a look at the city in general. The UAE's economy was booming at the time and, having sent my CV out to companies in advance of my two-week trip there, the offers of interviews came in thick and fast. It was clear it was an opportunity not to be missed, so from several offers I chose an agency and joined as account director and head of English language delivery.

In under six months of working for the PR agency, I had decided I would only be happy in my job doing things my own way, so was given the opportunity to establish the marketing communications department for a medium-sized advertising agency in the city, which I grabbed with both hands. Despite winning some impressive accounts, including Bosch and Sharaf DG within two years working in the position, I decided to move forward as a freelance consultant. It was during this period working as a freelancer in 2009 that I landed a role in Abu Dhabi, promoting the activations and education initiatives surrounding the city's first F1 Grand Prix. A huge success and fantastic experience, the position elevated my reputation within the industry and vastly improved my network. As part of the three-month project I recommended two event managers to come in and handle the launch press conference, then post-event convinced them to set up in partnership my first company - marketing agency, Custard Communications.

Custard Communications hit the ground running, winning some high-profile clients and capitalising upon some of the governmental relationships we had developed during the F1 project. However, with events being an area unsuitable long term for someone who struggles with multitasking, we split the agency into two where I continued to grow the PR side of the business, while the other partners concentrated solely on event management. By this point, I had won some high-profile integrated briefs, including Air Miles, Tim Hortons and FranklinCovey - helping well-known brands move towards digital communications, across PR, social media, mobile apps and online advertising. It was an exciting time in the marketing industry and the event management arm of the business was proving an unwelcome distraction, consuming time that should have been spent focusing on the real growth area of the business. Before long I couldn't see the benefit of being part of the company that I had started, so we dissolved the partnership in 2011 and I used my share to establish Integrated Holistic Communications (iHC), which continues to grow steadily to this day. With headquarters in Dubai and clients across several countries, I am now focused on developing the iHC brand internationally, winning business and helping the teams deliver integrated communications across a wide variety of sectors and brands.

In 2013, I took a year out from the Dubai office to create and lead a marketing department for a year-long project in London when hired as Head of Communications for the launch of an ambitious sport social media app called

Sportlobster. I quickly built a marketing team of 17 and had a large budget to utilise a wide variety of marketing activities, from PR to influencer marketing, online advertising, social media, outdoor, television, events and activations. We established an in-house influencer marketing team and ran campaigns around major global sporting events, optimising constantly and setting the company on the way to eventually driving over two million registrations over a two-year period, including helping the company raise in excess of £15m in venture capital in the process through the integrated marketing efforts. Throughout all that, I maintained the growth of iHC's team and client roster, while also keeping my hand in at writing, having been published across several different magazine titles and many times in the leading UAE newspaper, The National, for whom I wrote a weekly column for several months.

The agency in Dubai, where I am still highly invested on a daily basis, continues to grow, but I am now based in Rio de Janeiro, where we are delivering integrated communications across South America, with clients in Brazil, Peru and Mexico. The focus in South America is particularly on international English-speaking clients looking to promote their activities in the continent and Brazilian organisations looking to promote their businesses internationally. When not doing this, I am providing international consultancy, helping organisations elevate their brands and market themselves better. The super-talented integrated team in our ever-growing Dubai office continues to work hard together to win, service and retain a diverse array of clients, who benefit from the results we consistently deliver - largely using the disciplines covered in this book.

Contact the author

Follow the author for tips, blogs and news on Promoting Your Business 2020 and its December 2020 release, plus other writing already in the pipeline.

Ian Hainey is available for marketing consultations and speaking opportunities internationally, and can be contacted at: ih-c.com/promoting-your-business

Twitter: PYB_ian_hainey

Facebook: PYBianhainey

LinkedIn: promoting-your-business

Acknowledgements

I feel lucky to be able to rely upon the people that edited this book. I may well spend a part of nearly every day editing other people's writing, but it is an altogether different kettle of fish proofing your own work. Words you have been over several times - over weeks and months - can only be tackled by a fresh pair of eyes and I have a lot to thank the following people for, taking the time out of their own busy lives to spend so many hours going through this with a fine-tooth comb. Therefore, I would like to acknowledge everyone who took the time to go through every word with a fine-tooth comb, including Ryan, Richard, Adele, Vincent Christina and my parents. Sonia, for the patience as I tampered with her original alien artwork and turned it into the book cover that we both agree will split opinion, but not go unnoticed. Thanks to my wife, Paula, who has taken on more than her fair share of looking after our young kids over the last year to afford me some space to write this. Alexandra Saikkonen-Williams, for running the Dubai office so well, meaning I have had some time to concentrate more on writing. Marcus Taylor of Taylor Sterling Associates, who is also our top business development executive. Mike McLintock, who gave me a big career break with the UK police corporate communications job and also provided the encouragement to lead the team and win a prestigious national award. Dave Smith, who was briefly my mentor at the Evening Express and then I later became his boss, much to his amusement. Charles Currie, who supported all my wacky tourism PR ideas. And to Lynn Hainey, who was in it from the start of iHC as operations manager, gave up a lot for the business, holding things together as it grew from only a few clients into a multi-million-dollar international agency.

www.ingramcontent.com/pod-product-compliance
Lightning Source LLC
Chambersburg PA
CBHW051316220526
45468CB00004B/1367